Vital Signs of Life in Our Spirit

Homer L. Crothers, Ph.D.

Library of Congress Control Number 11094080611

Crothers, Homer L. 1939-
    Vital Signs of Life In Our Spirit ©/ by Homer L. Crothers, Ph.D.

ISBN 979-8-9855660-3-1

Cover, Chapter Preamble, and Header artwork by Tom Griffithe. The color blue honors the priestly garments described in Exodus 28:31-38.
Page vi   ID93558334 © R. Gino Santa Maria, Shutterfree, LLC, Dreamstime.com

I anoint this book with the healing power of God's love for each one who picks it up, reads it, and for each home in which it rests.

Dedicated to

Phil Dover

A colleague and friend of many years who has encouraged me to give the Word of the LORD to as many people as possible in every way possible.

This book is one of those ways.

Acknowledgement

Proverbs 15:22 states, *without counsel, plans go awry, but in the multitude of counselors they are established.* The work of this book has gone through some amazing reviews that have proven to be wise counsel. Among those counselors are my wife, Sandra, who has read every draft and asked the questions that helped me clarify points; my son, Kevin; daughter, Lori Ann; son-in-law, Brian; and sister Janice Lee, who knew how to find and correct my grammatical errors and pointed out places that needed more depth so the reader could clearly understand what I wanted to share.

I thank each of you for your dedication and assistance!

An incredibly special thanks to my brother in Christ Jesus, Tom Griffithe, for his insightful artwork for the cover, chapter preamble, and page headers. You accomplished what the Holy Spirit revealed to me regarding the blue preamble and header with light rays.

Thank you, Quintin McChristian, for your exceptional dedication in the information's completion of the back cover. You are the man to whom the Lord led me in a dream to design the Love Life Ministry website. Now you are my brother in Christ Jesus, who has helped me with this book.

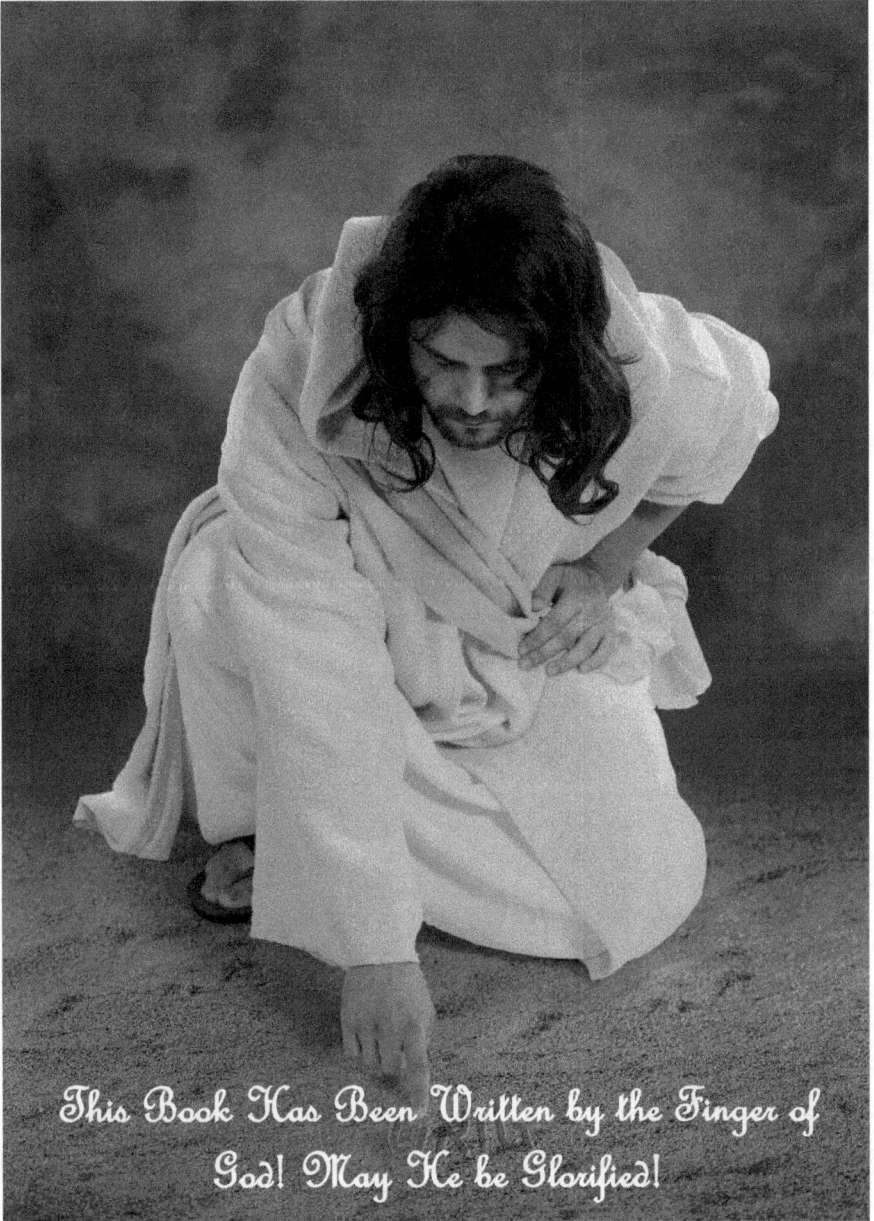

This Book Has Been Written by the Finger of God! May He be Glorified!

Psalm 71:18

Now also when I am old and gray-headed,
O God, do not forsake me,
Until I declare Your strength to this generation,
Your power to everyone who is to come.

TABLE OF CONTENTS

TABLE OF CONTENTS

INTRODUCTION

I had no intention or desire to write about the vital signs of life in our spirit. El Elyon, God Most High, my Abba Father, spoke to me in a dream during the early morning hours of August 9, 2021. In this dream, the Lord spoke to my mind about emergency room procedures in a hospital. His first focus was on the vital signs of life in our human body. His second focus was on the emergency room procedure. Then Abba told me to write about the vital signs of life in our spirit. I asked Him to teach me because I did not know of either those signs or the details of the vital signs of life in our human body. I believe I will use what I learn about the vital signs of life in our spirit in other situations in which Abba places me.

Abba is bringing forth what He taught me about the human body in my three years of pre-med biology studies. There are three primary vital signs of life in our human body. They are pulse rate, respiratory rate, and body temperature. When these three vital signs are measured, blood pressure is also measured. This fourth "vital sign" is not addressed in this writing because both the pulse rate and respiratory rate can influence blood pressure.

My objective, in this writing, is two-fold:

First, to fulfill Psalm 4:6 (NKJV), *there are many who say, "Who will show us any good?" LORD, lift up the light of Your countenance upon us.*

Second, to identify and describe equivalent vital signs of life in our spirit and relate them to the vital signs of life in our human body.

My approach is three-tiered.

First-tier provides a clear layman's understanding, to the reader, regarding the vital signs of their physical body. The information provided for the vital signs can be found in the text Human Anatomy, 2nd Edition by Michael McKinley and Valerie Dean O'Loughlin, McGraw-Hill Higher Education, 2008.

Second-tier addresses the significant parts of mankind drawing from various scriptures in the New King James Version Bible (NKJV).

Third-tier identifies the vital signs of our spirit life. These vital signs are linked to scripture from the New King James Version Bible. In addition, the identified vital signs of our spirit life come from Abba Father through my prayer conversations with Him. Matthews 7:7–8 states, *Ask, and it shall be given to you; seek and you will find; knock, and it will be opened to you. For everyone who asks receives, and he who seeks finds, and to him who knocks, it will be opened.*

Further, Philippians 4:6 tells us, *be anxious for nothing, but in everything by prayer and supplication, with thanksgiving, let your requests be made known to God; and the peace of God, which surpasses all understanding, will guard your hearts and minds through Christ Jesus.* In the Reflection, I relate the vital signs of the physical body and spirit life showing how crucial they are to one another in providing each person a victoriously satisfying life on this earth.

Our physical body is fearfully and wonderfully made (Psalm 139:14).

I pray each reader will be greatly blessed as they read this book.

I will praise You, for I am fearfully and wonderfully made!

Psalm 139:14

CHAPTER 1: Vital Signs of Life in Our Human Body

Pulse rate, respiratory rate, and body temperature[1] are measured by medical personnel in an emergency room, medical clinic, doctor's office, as well as paramedics attending an emergency situation to determine the status of the patient's life. These vital signs alert medical professionals to how close the patient is to living or dying.

Human Body Vital Sign 1: Pulse Rate

When a sperm from a man enters the ovum of a woman, life begins! In twelve weeks, the heart, arteries, vessels, and blood are functional. The sinoatrial node, in the heart, causes the heart to beat sixty to eighty times per minute. The heart beat and pulse rate are the same.[2]

Once the heart begins beating, it will not stop until there is either an external or internal adverse impact directly to the heart or to vital organs in the body. My heart has been beating for eighty-two years without stopping as of the time of this writing.

In the womb, the baby is kept alive by its own blood in its own cardiac system. The mother's blood does not enter the baby's vessels. A blood barrier in the mother's body near the placenta prevents a blood exchange and allows nutrients to leave the mother's blood and enter the baby's blood. Therefore, chemicals such as nicotine, alcohol, and drugs pass through the blood barrier into the baby's blood. In the opposite direction, waste from the baby's blood passes through the blood barrier into the mother's blood. That waste is removed from the mother's blood through her body functions.[3]

The blood in the cardiac system of the body performs critical life-sustaining functions. Blood carries deoxygenated blood to the lungs and returns freshly oxygenated blood to the body. Nourishment is carried by the blood from the digestive system throughout the body. The immune system functions within the vessels being transported to injured or infected areas located somewhere in the body. Thus, blood carries healing and recovery to needed areas of our body.[4]

LIFE IS IN THE BLOOD! (Leviticus 17:11)

Human Body Vital Sign 2: Respiratory Rate

Inhalation is inspiration, and exhalation is expiration. Together they are the primary function of the respiratory system through an exchange process which removes carbon dioxide from the blood, exchanging it for fresh oxygenated blood. Inhalation brings oxygen from the atmosphere into the lungs and diffuses it from the lungs into the blood within the cardiovascular system. Exhalation expels carbon dioxide from the blood into the atmosphere. This exchange is accomplished through the respiratory bronchioles, alveolar ducts, and alveoli. In the fourth week of pregnancy, the baby's respiratory diverticulum and primary bronchial buds have formed.[5]

By the sixth week, the tertiary bronchi of the left and right lungs have formed. After birth, the nasal cavity warms and humidifies inhaled air. The entrance to the nasal cavity is lined with course hairs called vibrissae to trap larger particles before they pass into the cavity. Within the trachea is a mucosa lining containing cilia to propel mucus ladened dust and dirt particles or other foreign matter toward the larynx and pharynx where it is swallowed.[6] These elements are the reason we cough.

After birth, the baby takes his or her first breath, causing the respiratory system to begin and continue to function. Once the lungs begin functioning with the first breath at birth, they will not stop until there is either an external or internal adverse impact directly on them or through an injury or illness in the body.

Dear reader, are you conscious of the air around you or concerned that there is enough air to keep you alive? Probably not! God, as our Abba Father, does not want us to be concerned about having enough air to breath. He created it for us so we could have life. In the same way that we depend upon air being there for us, we should be dependent upon Him for all of our needs. Philippians 4:19 gives us a promise that *God shall supply all your need according to His riches in glory by Christ Jesus.*

Human Body Vital Sign 3: Body Temperature

Thermoregulation is the control of body temperature. It is influenced by vast capillary networks and sweat glands in the dermis. While all arteries and vessels are crucial to the function of our body, dermal blood vessels have an important role in regulating body temperature. Vasoconstriction causes the blood vessels to narrow when the body is cold in order to conserve heat in the blood. Vasodilation causes blood vessels to increase so more blood can flow, and more body heat can be dissipated through the skin. Therefore, the blood in the human body regulates body temperature. Under normal conditions, body temperature is controlled between 97.4 and 97.9-degree Fahrenheit.[7]

Blood regulates body temperature in other ways. Blood plasma absorbs and distributes heat throughout the body. The acidity and alkalinity of the body tissues are kept in balance by blood plasma continuously, which, in turn, regulate body temperature. Antibodies in blood plasma are transported to injured and infected areas of the body. Such actions work to regulate body temperature.[8, 9]

Prior to the birth of a baby, the heart beats, and the body temperature is controlled at the proper level. However, should the mother experience an extreme change in her body temperature, such as falling into winter-cold icy water, her body will enter hypothermia shock. Such a condition can have an adverse impact on the baby in her womb because the blood loses heat rapidly.

Any one of the three vital signs, pulse rate, respiratory rate, and body temperature, when out of control, can result in death of the human body.

Now may the God of peace Himself sanctify you completely; and may your whole spirit, soul, and body be preserved blameless at the coming of our Lord Jesus Christ.

1 Thessalonians 5:23

CHAPTER 2: Significant Parts of Mankind

The term "mankind" is generic for man and woman who are human beings. In God's word, Job 12:10 refers to the life of every living thing and the breath of all mankind. James 3:2 confirms that mankind exercises control over every kind of animal life. Psalm 8:4–8 tells of God's relationship with mankind through His mindfulness of them, the glory and honor He gives to them, and the control of His creation He has imparted to them.

What cannot be explained by medical science is when the spirit of mankind enters the human body. Therefore, we must go to God's word provided in His Holy Scriptures, the Bible. The book of Genesis reveals how God created the universe and earth for mankind to inhabit. It further describes His creation of the environment, plants, and animal life that mankind would need while living on the earth. Genesis 1:26 and 2:7 states that God made mankind in His own image; in the image of God, He created male and female. God created man from the dust of the earth and breathed into his nostrils the breath of life. Genesis 2:21–22 states that God created a female by causing a deep sleep to come upon the man Adam. Then God drew a rib from Adam's side and closed the flesh. From the rib, God made woman. She became a helpmate to Adam. Thus, mankind, male and female, became living beings. While the woman, Eve, came from the man, Adam, all males and females will come from man through a woman. Therefore, I submit that in the womb, a male or female child is a human being at the beginning of conception and when the baby is born and takes his first breath, his spirit from God enters his body and he becomes a complete living being.

While people have apparent differences in their features and characteristics, there are three significant and distinctive parts to mankind. Drawing from 1 Thessalonians 5:23, we find that the whole person is a being of three parts: spirit, soul, and body. Hebrews 4:12 confirms that each person has a soul, spirit, joints, and marrow (body). We will look at each part separately.

Spirit

A baby is a human being at conception. The entrance of the spirit occurs when a baby takes her first breath, making her a complete living being. The spirit is our inner man, our true being. We are a spirit living in a physical body. John 4:24 states that God is a Spirit. Genesis 1:26 states that God made man in His image; therefore, since God is a Spirit, man is also a spirit because he is made in the image of God. Jeremiah 1:5 informs us that God knew us before He formed us in our mother's womb. Therefore, it is God who places our spirit in our physical body.

However, God wants us to have a clear understanding of who we are in the spirit or our inner man. He tells us in 1 Corinthians 2:14 that the natural man, we who are spirit, soul, and body, cannot receive the truth of the Spirit of God because in our natural state, we see God's words and declarations as being foolish. We are further taught, in 1 Corinthians 2:11, that a person knows the ways of another only through the spirit within him or her, and 1 Corinthians 2:10 informs us that God only reveals His ways to people through His Spirit.

So, what is the issue? Ephesians 2:1 tells us that in the beginning of our life, we are dead in trespasses and sins. The term "dead" in this passage means "being destitute of life"[10] so that we cannot recognize God or be devoted to Him because of the sin-filled nature of our spirit. 1 Corinthians 2:12 calls the sin-filled spirit a spirit of the world. That condition came upon all mankind when Adam, the first man, disobeyed God's instruction not to eat of the Tree of the Knowledge of Good and Evil. This was the only tree Adam was instructed not to eat. Adam made a decision outside his faith in God. All actions taken outside of faith in God are sin, for it says to God that we do not need Him. Actions outside of faith in God tell Him that we can do it ourselves. The problem is that we do not do it very successfully. Our action most often becomes our next problem.

The solution to this dilemma is found in Ephesians 3:16 where we are told that our spirit can be strengthened through the Holy Spirit. In John 10:10, we learn that Jesus came to give us life and life more abundantly. The unifying call is 2 Corinthians 6:2, which states, *"In an acceptable time I have heard you, and in the day of salvation I have helped you." Behold, now is the accepted time; behold now is the day of salvation.* Therefore, when we feel the touch of Jesus upon our heart, we are to receive Him as our Redeemer, Savior, and Lord.

Soul

The soul is our mind, will, and emotions. Medical science knows the location of man's brain and its function and capability. However, medical science does not know the location of man's mind, as shown by the following.

"Where does the mind reside? It is a question that has occupied the best brains for thousands of years. Now, a patient who is self-aware—despite lacking three regions of the brain thought to be essential for self-awareness—demonstrates that the mind remains as elusive as ever."[11]

"The philosophical neurosurgeon soon encounters difficulties when localizing the abstract concepts of mind and soul within the tangible 1300-gram organ containing 100 billion neurons."[12]"

Medical science knows that the mind is a tremendously strong and intelligent entity. It is known that the mind can influence the cells of the human body, causing them to become sick or to become healed.

"Contrary to a long philosophical tradition, it is particularly important to emphasize that the mind is not a 'substance' or *res*. If the mind were a substance its study would be beyond the empiricist domain of science and would belong to the extra empiricist domain of metaphysics. On the other hand, if the mind were a substance, it would be something individual. Nevertheless, the mind is a collection of various classes of processes that can be studied empirically. These processes are just the so-called "mental processes," in such a way that we can suggest the apparently vicious circle statement: mind is the collection of the different mental processes."[13]

"Philosophers have studied intelligence for centuries, but it is only in the last several decades that developments in a broad range of science and engineering fields have opened up a thriving "intelligence research" enterprise, making questions such as these approachable: How does the mind process sensory information to produce intelligent behavior?"[14]

Medical science knows that cells in the human body communicate with one another and with the mind.

"There are many different ways that cells can connect to each other. The three main ways for cells to connect with each other are: gap junctions, tight junctions, and desmosomes. These types of junctions have different purposes and are found in different places."[15]

"The average human brain contains about eighty-six billion nerve cells, called neurons. These are the building blocks of your brain. Neurons communicate with each other by sending chemical and electrical signals. Each neuron is connected with other neurons across tiny junctions called 'synapses"[16]

Therefore, mental stress and worry can communicate sickness to the cells in the body.[17]

"The idea that the mind can exert healing powers over the body is one that is most often associated with pseudoscience—and, usually, justifiably so. Cancer patients can't think their way to healthy; depression doesn't work like that, either. But, on the other hand, consider the placebo effect and the subjective improvement in symptoms people report after taking bogus drugs. Clearly, the mind and body work in tandem when it comes to our experience of some physical ailments."[18]

In 2014, Alex*[19], a young athlete, walked to the front of the church where my wife, Sandra, and I were standing. We were available to pray for anyone who came. Alex stated that he injured his right shoulder during a weight lifting workout. As we prayed over him, I touched his right shoulder and shoulder blade calling forth healing. We prayed over Alex for fifteen minutes and told him to see his shoulder healed. Then he said the pain was gone. Alex lifted his right hand over his head and lowered it. Then he rotated his shoulder. Both actions were accomplished without pain. Alex believed God's word to be true. In that truth, he placed his faith in God. God saw Alex's faith and healed his shoulder.

God confirms in Matthew 6:31 that worry is not good, for therein He states, *do not worry, saying, 'What shall we eat?' or 'What shall we drink?' or 'What shall we wear?' For all these things the Gentiles seek.* In Matthew 6:32, God also confirms that He knows all that we need, and if we will seek first His kingdom and His righteousness, all of what we need shall be given to us.

God led the Apostle Paul to teach and write in Romans 12:2 that people should not be conformed to this world, but they are to be transformed by renewing their mind. Renewing our mind by hearing, reading, and meditating on God's word in the Bible will show us the good and acceptable perfect will of God.

Isaiah 26:3 tells us that God will keep us in perfect peace when we set our mind on Him.

1 Peter 1:13 and 22 states that we should prepare our mind for action; therefore, we should think about what we are going to say before it is said.

On May 11, 2021, I submitted an online form to the Georgia Secretary of State for incorporation of Love Life Ministry. On May 21, 2021, I received a rejection because the company name cannot be used as an organizer name. I refiled the form with what I consider to be the correction only to be rejected on June 21, 2021. I went through the correction and refiling process again. After thirty days I did not receive a rejection letter and thought the corporation was completed. On October 12, 2021, the Holy Spirit led me to check for Love Life Ministry LLC on the Georgia Secretary of State listing. The name could not be found. I sent an email to the office after which I received a message, stating that the corporation of the organization was deemed to be abandoned. No further explanation was given. I allowed that statement to make me angry and replied to the office stating that the state employees were not interested, nor did they cared about those who try to navigate the Georgia state required protocol. If a form is not correct, a rejection letter is sent by an employee who thinks they have completed their duty. No offer of help is communicated to the one receiving the rejection letter. My reply was filled with condemnation. It was absent of kindness. After a few hours, I reconsidered my written outburst and asked Abba to help me with this issue. He led me to send another email asking for specific assistance, to which I received a reply stating I should send an email to the examiner named on the last rejection letter at the email address provided. I followed through with that suggestion, requesting specific assistance. There upon, I received specific instructions for the correction needed with a note stating that the "deemed abandoned" status had been changed to "rejection." Now, I could make the specific correction and refile without paying another $100 fee. Within fifteen minutes of refiling, I received a Certificate of Organization making Love Life Ministry an LLC.

I reflected on this situation and my earlier action, then I saw that Abba answered my prayer by telling me what to do and gave me favor with the examiner that resulted in not having to pay another $100 incorporating fee.

Abba cleared my spirit heart of loss and disappointment, then He restored me with joy as I praised Him for His help. Abba did not condemn me for my unkindness. He met my need so I could thank the state employee for their help and praise Him for loving and helping me.

Romans 7:5 states that our carnal mind will lead us to do what our flesh wants to do, but when we are spirit-minded, we will do what God leads us to do.

The carnal mind is enmity toward God. Enmity is a deep-seated hatred. Living life with a carnal mind is living in a state of death with vehement anger toward God.

Romans 8:5–7 supports Romans 7:5 by reminding us that our carnal mind is death, and the mind of Christ, the Spirit mind, is life and peace. It goes on to state that those who live according to their fleshy appetites will set their minds on things of the flesh.

When we accept Jesus as our Redeemer, Savior, and Lord, our spirit is made new and the mind of Christ, through the Holy Spirit, comes into our spirit. We still have a carnal mind, therefore, as stated in Romans 12:2, *we are not to be conformed to this world but be transformed by the renewing of our mind.* This transformation occurs as we, through the teaching and help of the Holy Spirit, strive to starve the carnal mind by living according to the Spirit setting our mind on things of the Spirit.

We can follow 1 Thessalonians 4:11 which encourages us to aspire to lead a quiet life minding our own business and work with our hands. God teaches us in Colossians 3:23 that the work we do with our hands should be done heartily as to the Lord and not to men; knowing that we will receive blessings from God. Further, Proverbs 16:3

confirms that we should commit our work to the Lord, and He will establish our thoughts. God's love for us and His generosity toward us is so great that He set a promise for us in 3 John 1:2 saying He wants us to prosper in all things and be in good health as our soul (mind, will, and emotions) prospers.

Body

Our body is the house in which our spirit lives. 1 Corinthians 6:19 reminds us that our body is the temple of the Holy Spirit. However, there is a condition. One must receive Jesus as Redeemer, Savior, and Lord, thereby accepting His sacrifice on the cross as payment for the sin we inherited from Adam.

At the time I wrote this, Abba showed me a man who has cancer but does not know it. I saw prostate cancer. If you are the man reading this, I reach out and touch you with the healing power of God's love. Abba made your body to be free of sickness. The enemy, Satan, intends to fill your body with sickness. I bless you with Abba's words, *by His stripes you are healed* (1 Peter 2:24). Now, may the God of hope fill you with all joy and peace in believing so that you may receive His healing power of love.

In August 2007, I had interstitial cystitis of the bladder that required medication for the remainder of my life. Away from home, I searched for restrooms. In October 2008, Robert, a Christian brother, prayed healing over me. The next day I stopped taking the medication. Over the next four years I experienced episodes of pain but stood against it in Jesus' name without medication. In 2012 all pain and restroom searches stopped.

According to Romans 12:1, we are to present our body as a living sacrifice, holy and acceptable to God. Before such a presentation can be made, we must have a new spirit by accepting Jesus as the Son of the Living God.

Thus, Jesus becomes our Redeemer, Savior, and Lord. Our body is the same before and after we accept Jesus. The fact is that each of us came from our earthly father through our earthly mother which makes our body acceptable to God, for it was He who designed and created the process. It was God who told Adam and Eve to be fruitful and multiply.

After we accept Jesus as our Redeemer, Savior, and Lord, we see our body differently than we did when we, as a spirit, were sin-filled. The difference is the presence of the Holy Spirit, who comes to dwell within our body alongside us as spirit to Spirit, making us *one spirit with Him* (1 Corinthians 6:17).

How do we present our body as a living sacrifice? First, we must consider that our body is a living entity. Our body is seen by others in this physical realm. No one sees us as a spirit, only that we are a living human being. It is we, the spirit, who must present our body as holy and acceptable.

Second, we are shown in Matthew 6:22, that our eyes are a lamp to our body. What we see can be good or bad. As we look at either good or bad, that image is implanted in our spirit-heart and our mind. It is implanted because we receive by choice what we see. When we see bad and receive it, instead of speaking against it, we make a choice to receive the bad. Each choice or action we make has a consequence. While we can choose what we want to see or the action we want to take, we cannot choose the consequence. It is through the free will that God has given us whereby we make choices. If the choice or action brings unwanted consequence, we cannot blame anyone else. When Adam made the choice to eat the fruit from the Tree of the Knowledge of Good and Evil and found himself naked and afraid, he blamed Eve saying to God, *The woman whom You gave to be with me, she gave me of the tree, and I ate.* In turn, Eve said, *"The serpent deceived me, and I ate* (Genesis 3:12–13). See how the blame game started, and it continues today. Of course, the serpent could not say anything because he did not have a leg to stand on.

According to Mark 7:20–21, Jesus taught that what comes out of the heart can defile us, such as evil thoughts, adultery, murder, theft, wickedness, and pride. Those characteristics can be seen in our actions and demeanor and heard in the words we speak. Those actions, demeanor and words defile us. Thus, we are to guard what our eyes see in order to present our body holy and acceptable to God through the Holy Spirit who lives beside us in our body.

Therefore, our eyes have an influence on our body, for Matthew 6:22, states that *if our eyes see good, our whole body will be filled with light. But if our eyes see bad, our whole body will be filled with darkness.*

Third, we learn through the reading of Romans 7:23, that every action taken, or word spoken outside faith in God is a sin. This teaching is expanded in 1 Corinthians 6:18, where we learn that when we commit sexual immoral sin, it is against our own body. On this point, I want to clarify that any sexual action outside of the marriage covenant is an immoral sin. Therefore, 1 Corinthians 6:19–20, teaches us that *our body is the temple of the Holy Spirit, who is in us, whom we have received from God, and that we are not our own. We were bought at a price; therefore, we are to glorify God in our body and in our spirit.*

Fourth, according to 1 Timothy 6:17, *God gives us richly all things to enjoy.* God gives to us generously. God gives all things. How much is all? It is the whole of His creation, and He gives it to us to enjoy. Even our eating and drinking, according to 1 Corinthians 10:31, is to be done to the glory of God.

The generosity of God can lead to over indulgence from which our body can be overburdened with excess weight or addiction. Burdening our body with excess weight or an addiction goes against the presentation of our body as holy and acceptable to God. How can such excess be the glory of God? Such over indulgence is not to the glory of God! It is to the glory of our fleshly appetite, which is a form of idolatry.

But God shows us how to glorify Him through our eating and drinking. In Galatians 5:22–23, God has listed nine fruits of the Holy Spirit, which are characteristics for us to demonstrate. One of those characteristics is self-control. Therefore, as we eat and drink to the glory of God, we are to practice self-control. When we rely on ourselves to practice self-control we often fail because will power only lasts a short time. Self-control is a fruit of the Holy Spirit; therefore, we must depend upon Him to help us stand against over indulgence in eating and drinking. In relying on the Holy Spirit, we are relying upon God's grace to provide all that we need.

Further, over indulgence in eating and drinking is a sickness for some people. They cannot heal that sickness alone. Jesus took whippings from the Roman soldiers so the stripes He received from that beating would be our healing and wholeness.

Each believer should partake of the Holy Communion daily declaring that they are healed and made whole by the stripes that Jesus took, and they are righteous by His blood shed during the beating and when nailed to the cross.

When we look at the amazing functionality of our body, Psalm 139:14 becomes true. W*e are fearfully and wonderfully made.*

I will give them a
heart to know Me,
for I AM the Lord;
and they will be My
people, and I will be
their God, for they
will return to Me
with their whole
heart.

Jeremiah 24:7

CHAPTER 3: Our Spirit Heart

In CHAPTER 1, I stated that twelve weeks after life begins in the womb, a heart, arteries, vessels, and blood are functional. Our spirit has a heart just as our physical body has a physical heart.

In CHAPTER 2, I submitted that when a baby takes his first breath his spirit enters his body making him a complete living being. The spirit is our inner man, our true being. We are a spirit living in a physical body.

Also, in CHAPTER 2, I stated that we have a soul, which is our mind, will, and emotions. At birth, the state of our mind is carnal. A carnal mind is one that has a strong focus on fleshly appetites. It is easily led by the world's temptations of the flesh. The carnal mind has enmity, which is a deep-seated hatred, toward the Spirit of God.

Further, in CHAPTER 2, I shared that Romans 8:5–7 reminds us that our carnal mind is death, and the mind of Christ, the Spirit mind, is life and peace. That scripture continues its teaching by stating that those who live according to their fleshy appetites will set their minds on things of the flesh. Those who live according to the Spirit will set their mind on things of the Spirit.

If the carnal mind comes to us through our spirit at birth, from where does the mind of Christ, the

Spirit mind of life and peace, come? The mind of Christ comes from Jesus giving us life and life more abundantly when we feel His touch upon our spirit heart. It is at that very moment we are to receive Him as our Redeemer, Savior, and Lord. Upon that act, the mind of Christ enters our spirit, and we are born again by the Spirit.

Where is our spirit heart located? The Hebrew word for heart is "leb," which is the same word for thoughts.[20] Therefore, I submit that "leb" means heart and mind. Recalling that medical science knows where the heart and brain are located in the body begs the question about the location of each in the spirit. The spirit-heart and mind, I offer, are at the center of our spirit.

What is the purpose of our spirit heart? Our spirit heart is a depository for those things our eyes see, ears hear, and the thoughts that enter our mind.

There are three sources of thoughts. They come from the Holy Spirit, Satan, who is the adversary, or from our human fleshy appetites. The only thoughts we should allow access to our spirit heart are those from the Holy Spirit. His thoughts will lift us, teach us wisdom, and give us peace and abundant life. His thoughts should fill our spirit heart.

Thoughts from the adversary are always condemning, negative, and oppressive because he wants to steal our peace, kill our life, and remove us from this earth. Human fleshly thoughts open the door to Satan, which we should keep tightly closed. Matthew 6:22–23 teaches us to avoid fleshly appetites by stating that, *the lamp of the body is the eye. If your eye is good, your whole body will be full of light. But, if your eye is bad, your whole body will be full of darkness. If the light in you is darkness, how great will be that darkness.* Being careful about what we see keeps our spirit-heart clean.

What is the function of our spirit heart? The primary function of our spirit heart is to feed the mind what will be thought then spoken by our mouth. According to Matthew 15:18, Jesus taught His disciples about the spirit heart saying, *things which proceed out of the mouth come from the heart, and they defile a man. For out of the heart proceed evil thoughts, murders, adulteries, fornications, thefts, false witness, blasphemies. These are things which defile a man.*

So, how do we keep defiled things from going into our heart? Philippians 4:8 provides an answer. We are to think and meditate on things that are true, noble, just, pure, lovely, of good report, virtue, and praiseworthy. We are to meditate on these things because they are characteristics of Jesus, and they bring peace to us.

We are to stand guard over what our eyes see, ears hear, and mind thinks. We are to practice self-control, which is a fruit of the Holy Spirit, who helps us stop worldly things we see and hear, and thoughts of the flesh from entering our spirit-heart.

In the 1980s, I traveled to Ireland often on business. On one of those trips, I stayed in the City of Galway at the Galway Hotel on the square. After working at a facility in the town of Loughrea, Ireland, about a twenty minute drive from Galway, I returned to the hotel for dinner and rest. At the time I wanted to have dinner, I left my room and walked to the lift. There I pressed the descend button and waited. The lift arrived, the door opened, and I saw that it was empty. Pressing the ground floor button, I stepped back to wait for the ride to stop. The ride was short, for the lift stopped at the floor below mine. After the door opened, an attractive Irish woman stepped onto the lift. Upon beginning the descent again, the woman asked where I was going. I replied, "To dinner." Arriving at the ground floor, the door opened and upon departing from the lift, the woman told me she was going to the pub and invited me to join her. I politely declined, turned, and walked to the dining room. The hostess placed me at a table that was positioned in the center of the dining area. Other tables flanked me on the left, right, and behind. After selecting my choice of dinner, it was

49

about an hour before I finished. Suddenly, the woman from the lift appeared at my table. She invited me to join her in the pub after I finished my meal. I said that I had work to complete in my room. She turned to leave and looking back said, "I will wait for you." Now I was in a fix that was not so fine. If I left my table, then, the other people in the dining area, who heard her invitation, might think I was going to join her. So, I summoned the server and ordered a dessert and coffee. These I consumed slowly, thinking about how I was going to avoid this woman. The pub was on the opposite side of the lift with full view of the lift from the pub. After eating my dessert and drinking my coffee, I stood to leave, convinced that the other diners would not think that I was going to join the woman in the pub. As I walked toward the lift, I said, "Lord give me clear passage to the lift and to enter it without the woman seeing me." Arriving at the lift, I turned my back to the pub and pressed the button. To my pleasant surprise, the door opened immediately. The lift was empty, and I hurried onto it and pressed my floor button. The door closed without an encounter with this woman. As I sat alone in my room and recalled this experience, I could see the strong temptations of the world being presented to me multiple times. All I had to do was respond in the affirmative. But, as Joseph, the son of Jacob said when he stood before Potiphar's wife who was trying to seduce him, I thought *how can I do this great wickedness, and sin against God?* (Genesis 39:9).

Our spirit heart is blessed when we do not walk according to the counsel of the ungodly world or stand with those who live by the flesh. As we guard our spirit heart, thus keeping the ungodly world out, God sees us as one who is like *a tree planted by the rivers of water, that brings forth its fruit in its season, whose leaf also shall not wither; and whatever he does shall prosper* (Psalm 1:1–3).

In Luke 6:43–45 is the account of Jesus teaching His disciples using a tree as a teaching aid. Therein He states that *a good tree does not bear bad fruit, nor does a bad tree bear good fruit.* He further states that a *tree is known for its fruit.* Jesus finishes His teaching by relating the tree and its fruit to man. Verse forty-five states, *a good man out of the good treasure of his heart brings forth good; and an evil man out of the evil treasure of his heart brings forth evil.* Then Jesus completes His teaching, in verse forty-five, with the operative theme, *for out of the abundance of the heart his mouth speaks.*

In reflecting on fruitfulness, I am reminded of a friend who shared how much it refreshed her to work in her garden. Then I thought of an apple. Man can count the seeds in an apple, but only God knows how many apples are in a seed. Likewise, God knows how fruitful each of us can be. Our fruitfulness is dependent upon John 15:5 where Jesus tells us *He is the vine, and we are the branch. Apart from Him, we can do nothing that is of worthy fruitfulness* (John 15:5–8).

Our spirit heart is as crucial to our life as our physical heart is to our human body. When our physical heart stops and cannot be revived, our human body dies. When our spirit heart is filled with the flesh of the world, our spirit, our inner man, lives in death.

Did you notice that statement? Our spirit does not die! Rather, it lives in death. That death can be removed, and the spirit revived when we call upon Abba Father in Jesus' name to restore us. John 11:25–26 confirms by Jesus' words that those who believe in Him, though they die physically shall live spiritually. Then Jesus asks a question, "Do you believe this?"

Ephesians 2:1–3, confirms that those who are not born-again already have a spirit heart that is living in death for it states, *we were dead in trespasses and sins, in which we once walked according to the course of this world, according to the prince of the power of the air (Satan), the spirit who now works in the sons of disobedience, conducting ourselves in the lusts of our flesh, fulfilling the desires of the flesh and of the mind.*

As people grow from infancy through childhood into adulthood, there are many opportunities to hear about Jesus and that His sacrifice has already paid for the sin they were born into. Yet, people reject Jesus as Redeemer, Savior, and Lord, saying they do not need Him or do not believe there is a God. At that point, regardless of the person's age, there is no salvation, only a sin-filled spirit heart exists. Rejection comes to people of all ages and in many forms. It comes from the secular side of life and the religious side. When my wife Sandra was a first-grader she asked a few girls if she could play with them. One of the girls said, "No!" Sandra asked why she could not play, and the girl said, "You are dirty!" Sandra replied that she had taken a bath. The girl grabbed her arm and rubbed it vigorously with her finger then said, "See, you are dirty!"

Jesus described a scene in Matthew 11:16, where children called to their companions saying they played the flute for them, but their companions did not dance. This scripture is in reference to the people who rejected *Jesus as the Son of Man calling Him a winebibber and glutton, a friend of tax collectors and sinners.*

Rejection is often spoken or demonstrated by a person who has a lack of knowledge. For example,

53

people who do not know God seek help from the world. They reach out to someone or an organization they can see or touch, but when the help or assistance they are seeking does not come or comes but does not meet their need, they reject the person or organization from which they sought help.

The scripture in Hosea 4:6 confirms the fact that *people are destroyed for lack of knowledge.* Sometimes a root of bitterness enters a person's spirit heart because they have experienced rejection by another, or they have been disappointed that what was promised did not come to reality. Hebrews 12:15 warns about a root of bitterness saying, *look carefully lest any root of bitterness spring up causing trouble and by this many become defiled.*

While rejection may be a cause of not accepting Jesus as Redeemer, Savior, and Lord, an unbeliever does not have to remain in a state of sin-filled existence. If they confess with their mouth that Jesus is the Son of the living God and believe in their heart that God raised Him from the dead, they will be saved (Romans 10:9). Their spirit will be made new. The state of death will leave their spirit making them new through the sacrifice of Jesus (2 Corinthians 5:17). All who receive Jesus as Redeemer, Savior, and Lord, are restored from death to life.

The next step after receiving Jesus as Redeemer, Savior, and Lord is becoming mature in our spirit heart. There are five levels of maturity for our spirit heart, which grows through stages of living.

Maturity Level 1

At the first maturity level of the spirit heart, we are born again having received Jesus as Redeemer, Savior, and Lord. At the moment of receiving Jesus, we become a new creation in Him. 2 Corinthians 5:17 confirms, *if anyone is in Christ, he is a new creation; old things have passed away; behold, all things have become new.* New believers are joyful and eager to share Jesus and what they experienced in receiving Him as their Redeemer, Savior, and Lord. They are hungry to read God's word and worship Him through praise music in a gathering of other believers. After a while, the world's pressures, distractions, and temptations brought by the devil through peer pressure draw many new believers away from their faith in God. They step off of God's path onto the world's path and experience drugs, alcohol, sex, and other illicit forms of living. For some, this journey on the wrong side continues for years. However, the salvation they received through accepting Jesus as their Redeemer, Savior, and Lord is not removed. Romans 8: 38–39 tells us that *neither death nor life, nor angels nor principalities nor powers, nor things present nor things to come, nor height nor depth, nor any other created thing, shall be able to separate us from the love of God which is in Christ Jesus our Lord.*

When someone returns to the Lord from the wrong side, there is a tendency to feel condemned for their time of wayward living. Romans 8:1 tells us that *there is now no condemnation to those who are in Christ Jesus, who do not walk according to the flesh, but according to the Spirit.* Notice that the scripture states *those who are in Christ Jesus,* not those who return to Christ Jesus. Even in a wayward illicit living, Jesus is with us. We do not sense His presence because we are focused on the lifestyle we adopted.

Those who do not go into a wayward illicit lifestyle can live in the world without sensing the presence of Jesus because they are extremely focused on what they want to do without regard to what God has planned for them to do.

Living a wayward illicit life or just living in the world without regard to God's plan for us has a negative impact on our spirit heart. In those situations, what we see, hear, and say goes into our spirit heart. It is evidenced by what comes out of our spirit heart through our actions and words spoken. Turning away from the wayward illicit life and returning to Jesus allows Him to cleanse our spirit heart. The journey toward full maturity of the spirit-heart begins with the new believer seeing himself as described in 2 Corinthians 5:17. This journey is a daily effort, but it is easy when we believe and accept that the work of maturity in our spirit heart is the work of God not our work.

Maturity Level 2

The second maturity level of the spirit heart is where the new believer feeds on the milk of God's word. The Apostle Paul said to the Corinthians, *I could not speak to you as spiritual people but as to carnal, as to babes in Christ. I fed you with milk and not with solid food because you were not able to receive it.* When we are born again, the mind of Christ enters our spirit. However, we still have a carnal mind, which lusts after the appetites of the flesh. The carnality in which the Corinthians were living was evident in their envy, strife, and divisions among them (1 Corinthians 3:1–5). Paul continued to lead the Corinthians from immaturity to maturity when he stated, *Brothers and sisters, stop thinking like children. In regard to evil be infants, but in your thinking be adults.* (1 Corinthians 14:20 NIV).

Hebrew 5:13 states, *for everyone who partakes only of milk is unskilled in the word of righteousness, for he is a babe*. What is *unskilled in the word of righteousness*? In the Thayer's Greek-English Lexicon, righteousness means equity of character.[21] Equity of character is how we live our life. The words we speak and the actions we take reflect the equity of our life, which are the characteristics justices, fairness, and uprightness.[22]

Partaking only of milk relates to how God sees us as infants. He uses the same procedure for born-again infants as he designed for human infants. Solid food cannot be given to babies at the infant stage because they do not know how to chew and swallow it, nor can their digestive system process it. Instead, babies are fed a mother's breast milk or formula milk. Babies instinctively know how to suck and swallow milk. Similarly, born-again infants, regardless of their age when they accept Jesus as Redeemer, Savior, and Lord, require the less difficult truths of the Christian belief. The less difficult truths begin with the understanding that a new believer still has the carnal mind with which they were born. Their carnal mind thinks that the truths of God's word are foolish. The evidence of that fact lies in the episodes of envy, strife, and divisions in which the new believer finds himself.

In this second level of maturity, new believers learn the old characters they should put off and the new characters to put on. Going to Colossians 3:5–17 we find a list of such characters. Some characters to put off include evil desires, covetousness, idolatry, anger, wrath, and filthy language. Some characters to put on include tender mercies, kindness, humility, forgiving one another, love, and allowing the peace of God to rule in our heart.

An example of putting off an old character is recorded in Luke 18:18–23. Therein, a rich young ruler is described as one who came to Jesus asking what he must do to inherit eternal life. Jesus asked the rich young ruler if he knew the commandments to which he answered that he kept the commandments *Do not commit adultery, Do not murder, Do not steal, Do not bear false witness*, and *Honor your father and your mother*. Whereupon Jesus seeing that the rich young ruler was proud of his accomplishment said to him, *You still lack one thing. Sell all that you have and distribute to the poor, and you will have treasure in heaven; and come, follow me.* When the rich young ruler heard Jesus' words, he turned and walked away sorrowfully for he was extraordinarily rich, and those riches had become his god.

I want to clarify that Jesus was not condemning the riches held by the young ruler. He was pointing out to him that his riches were a hinderance to achieving what he sought—eternal life. Jesus confirms in Luke 18:24 the hinderance of riches by saying, *How hard it is for those who have riches to enter the kingdom of God!*

Further, Jesus gives an analogy of the difficulty that a rich person could experience in wanting to enter the kingdom of God by saying, *it is easier for a camel to go through the eye of a needle than for a rich man to enter the kingdom of God*. But Jesus further clarifies that riches do not make it impossible for someone to enter the kingdom of God by saying, *the things which are impossible with men are possible with God*. When Jesus told the rich young ruler to give his riches to the poor, He wanted the man to live his life in a relationship with Him where he could look to God to provide all his needs instead of depending upon his wealth.

The first part of Proverbs 11:28 teaches that whoever trusts in their riches will fail. The reason for such failure is shown in 1 Timothy 6:10, *the love of money is a root of all kinds of evil, for which some have strayed from the faith in greediness and pierced themselves through with many sorrows*. The second part of Proverbs 11:28 teaches that the righteous will have a good effect on people around them and succeed at what they do. Therefore, it is the righteous who live a life that reflects their equity of character. No one earns their way into eternal life through accumulation of wealth or by work. Being rich or poor is not a prerequisite for inheriting eternal life. Jesus paid the full price for mankind's inheritance of eternal life. The price paid was for everyone. It is likened to receiving a gift with our name on it. In order to have the gift, we must open the package and accept it.

The following scriptures provide new believers a solid foundation upon which to learn about and come to understand God's character and the basic principles that support their faith. Take time to read the following scriptures before continuing this book.

John 14:6, Jesus is the only way!
1 John 1:5–9, God is light, He removed sin, He is faithful!
2 Corinthians 5:17, in Christ, we are a new creation; the old has passed away!
Ephesians 2:8, by faith we have been saved, not by the works we do!
Galatians 5:16–25, walk in the Spirit, not in the flesh to fulfill its desires!
Psalm 119:9–11, hide God's word in our heart!
Ephesians 6:10–20 suit up for the battle!

Philippians 4:6–7, settle it in our heart not to be anxious, but to be in God's peace!
1 Corinthians 13:4–8, how God loves us so we can love others!
Matthew 28:18–20, share our good experience and good news with others!

In 1 Corinthians 1:30, we learn that God has made Jesus to be wisdom for us. As we worship the LORD in a quiet place of our own or in a church setting, that worship is the beginning of knowledge (Proverbs 1:7) and the beginning of wisdom (Psalm 111:10). Good biblical teaching increases the knowledge of God, which leads to full maturity of our spirit heart. Therefore, each believer should attend a local church where Jesus is exalted. A church where the teaching is about what He has done to give us our salvation, which is underserved, unmerited, unearned grace, not about law. Teaching law is about the works we must do to keep our salvation.
The milk of God's word we hear from attending a local church and reading the Holy Bible strengthens and encourages our spirit heart so we can continue the journey toward full maturity.

Maturity Level 3
At the third maturity level of the spirit heart, we begin feeding on the solid food of God's word. At this level, we grow in the understanding of God's

word to the point that we refuse the world's wisdom and speak the wisdom of God, which is hidden but is revealed to us through the Holy Spirit (1 Corinthians 2:6).

We learn that in our reverence of the LORD, the Holy Spirit reveals knowledge (Proverbs 1:7) and wisdom (Psalm 111:10) to us. Further we learn in Proverbs 8:12 that *wisdom dwells with prudence and finds knowledge and discretion.* The Holy Spirit revealed to me the depth of this teaching, which means wisdom comes with careful thinking and implementation of actions while incorporating experiential learning and facts, then behaving and speaking without causing offense or revealing private information.

Further, we learn at this third maturity level to place a confidently assured trust in God that His way is the best direction for us. Therefore, we lean upon Him and not upon our own understanding (Proverbs 3:5). Through this confidently assured trust in God, we learn to acknowledge Him in the things we do, thereby He makes our path straight, easy, and successful (Proverbs 3:6).
As we continue to have a confident trust in God, He begins to communicate with us through dreams and visions. Joel 2:28 confirms this by stating, *your old men shall dream dreams, your young men shall see visions.*

At the time of writing this, I was a young eighty-two year old man. I learned that it is a good practice to record the date and time when the dreams and visions come to us for it is through those events that God tells or shows us what He is going to do in our life or the life of another person. Therefore, we will have a record that confirms the completion of the dream or vision.

In the early morning hours of November 6, 2021, I was in prayer, praying in the Spirit, when the following vision came before my eyes. I saw myself as a human body cell with two channels through the membrane. One channel was through the membrane on the right side and the other was through the membrane on the left. Above me and to my right, I saw Jesus. A pipe was connected to the channel on the right side of my membrane and connected to Jesus. Healing power flowed through the pipe from Jesus going through the channel on the right side and continuing through me to the channel on the left, then flowing into the person for whom I was touching and praying to be healed.

Seeing myself as a body cell gave me a reference to the membrane of the cells in our body. The membrane is the outside of the cell like our skin is the outside of our body. Inside each cell is a nucleus and organelles which maintain the cell's life and the life of our body.[23] In order to nourish the cell and sustain life, there are channels and transporters in the membrane of the cell. Minerals such as potassium (K+) and nitrogen (N+) flow through the channels from the cell into the cytoplasm and back into the cell.[24] The purpose for the comparison of my body to a cell was to give me an image of how God's healing power will come from Jesus into me and through me into the person for whom I am praying and touching to be healed.

When I saw Jesus, in the vision, I saw a menorah, which is a lamp stand with seven lamps. Exodus 25:31–39 describes the menorah to have a center lamp with three lamps on each side. It was used in the Hebrew tabernacle to provide light for the priests serving in the Holy Place. The lamps were arranged so each would give its light in front of it. The Hebrew priests added fresh olive oil to the bowls of each lamp daily to keep them burning from evening to morning. In my vision, Jesus was the center lamp of the menorah with three on each side. The healing power flowing from Jesus through the pipe to me was a continual flow like the olive oil is provided continually to the lamps of the menorah.

Having dreams and visions shows that the maturity of our spirit heart is increasing. The most exciting attribute of this growth in maturity is that God is building a strong stable intimate relationship with us. We grow as His son or daughter from infancy to adulthood. In the growth of this relationship, we see God as our Abba Father, which is to say, Daddy God!

Maturity Level 4

At the fourth maturity level of the spirit heart, we learn to walk in faith with God as our Abba Father. Such a walk of faith becomes a lifestyle. We understand and accept that most times we must step out in faith when it seems there is nothing to step on. In this step of faith, we believe that Abba will place a stable and secure foundation under our feet. Further, we know that there will be times when we allow a misspoken word to escape our mouth or take an action that should have been kept under guard. In such times as these, we will not be condemned. Instead, we remember that we are righteous, and Jesus has already paid for our mistake. There will likely be words of repentance spoken to Abba, indicating that we have changed our mind and direction 180 degrees from where we made our mistake. We see the mistake as a learning opportunity thanking the Holy Spirit for teaching us the way in which we should go.

As we live in this fourth maturity level of our spirit heart, we find a hunger to sit in quiet prayer and meditation with Abba. Sometimes we make our requests known to Him. At other times we simple sit quietly in His Presence allowing Him to speak with us. Through these quiet times, we come to an understanding and acceptance that our life should be regulated one day at a time. Yesterday has gone and tomorrow has not arrived.

Therefore, we do not worry about tomorrow, for tomorrow will worry about its own things. Sufficient for the day is its own trouble (Matthew 6:34).

As we live in each day, our conversation should be with the Holy Spirit, who abides within us alongside our spirit. We should seek His help with something we are doing or ask for His guidance regarding a decision we must make or request an answer to a question or to resolve a problem. In our conversation with the Holy Spirit, we may pray in tongues, if we had asked for and received the baptism of the Holy Spirit. It has been my experience that when I have gone to Abba in prayer and a barrier or force seemed to stand between us, I would pray in the Spirit, in tongues. Praying in tongues brought peace and removed the barrier or force, then my conversation with the Holy Spirit continued unhindered. 1 Corinthians 14 provides much information regarding speaking in tongues. Some people have stated that speaking in tongues is of the devil. How can the scriptures of the Holy Bible, God's word, contain anything of the devil? It cannot! Jude 20 states, B*ut you, beloved, building yourselves up on your most holy faith, praying in the Holy Spirit.*

In this fourth level, we experience a mature spirit heart that is pure because we see and believe, thus Jesus said, *blessed are the pure in heart, for they shall see God* (Matt. 5:8). **Who** are the pure in heart? Those whose heart has been purified by faith, which is believing. The Hebrew word for faith is Emunah, which also means belief.[25] The Greek word for faith is Pistis and for believe is Pistueo.[26]

As we live in the fourth maturity level of our spirit heart, we find an exceedingly abundant flow of blessings from our Abba. It is an excitingly wonderful time.

I am reminded of being a boy at Christmas. My dad would walk me to the town square in Cumberland, Maryland. The city hall building was a large square with a landscape border around it. The sellers of fresh-cut Christmas trees would have them tied with twine and leaning against the building. My job was to select the Christmas tree for our house to be enjoyed by myself, my mother, younger brothers, and sister. It took me a long time to select a tree. It had to be tall and the trunk straight so it would stand proudly inside our house. My dad was patient as I walked around the city hall building many times.

Our Abba is also very patient with us as we walk with Him or sit quietly with Him. He takes great pleasure in providing what He knows will make us happy. As Philippians 4:19 states, *my God shall supply all your need according to His riches in glory by Christ Jesus*. And Psalm 23:1 confirms for us that *the LORD is my shepherd; I shall not want*.

Shari *[27], a Christian sister, told me of an encounter she experienced after leaving Home Depot in Newnan, Georgia. There she met a struggling veteran. He was nearing homelessness and was in the parking lot washing car windows for money. Shari told the veteran she was not able to give him any money. Instead, she offered him a job. As Shari spoke with the veteran, she learned that he had been injured in action and was not able to take the job due to losing his disability payment. He told Shari that his prayers had been answered by her stopping and talking with him. The veteran was grateful for her visit. Shari said, "Today, I was exactly where I needed to be in order to bless someone."

Dear reader, this experience shows how we can easily live in the fourth maturity level of our spirit heart.

Maturity Level 5

At the fifth maturity level of the spirit heart, we learn how to live with God in an intimate way. This intimacy begins with knowing the substance of Jesus. His substance is His inherent, unchanging nature, His essence, His love! There are many accounts in the Holy Bible that provide word picture examples of Jesus' substance. In one account, those who ate the bread and fish He multiplied tasted Jesus' love. Psalm 34:8 states, *Oh, taste and see that the LORD is good.*

Another account describes a woman who had a twelve-year-old bleeding issue. When she went into the crowd that had formed around Jesus and quietly touched the hem of his garment, she felt the healing power of Jesus' love. This account can be read in Luke 8:43–48.

Then there is an account in John 9:1–7 of a man born blind who lived his entire life in darkness. When Jesus and His disciples were in the presence of the man, His disciples asked Him if the man or his parents sinned, which caused his blindness. Jesus replied that neither the man nor his parents sinned. The condition was an opportunity for all to see the healing power of God's love. Jesus supported His statement by taking soil to which He added His saliva making a mud. Then He placed the mud upon the man's eyes and instructed him to go wash in the pool of Siloam, which means Sent. The man obeyed and came back seeing for the first time in his life. The man saw Jesus' love.

These examples show that we can taste, feel, and see the LORD. All these people had hoped for something. Our spoken hope for what we desire is the key that opens the door to Jesus' love, His substance. A state of hopelessness is a lost key.

As we grow into the fifth maturity level of the spirit heart, the substance of Jesus becomes real in our life. I am experiencing this growth. On November 20, 2021, as I was settling onto my bed for sleep, I was aware that I was settling into Jesus. I could see His Presence enveloping me. It was as if His Presence moved to cover my arms and legs. The enveloping did not completely cover me. This experience occurred again on December 1, 2021, as I was settling onto my bed to sleep. At that time, I was aware that I was settling into Abba Father. I could see His Presence moving toward my arms and legs as I sank into Him. The enveloping did not completely cover me. When I returned to bed after going to the bathroom or getting a drink of water, I was aware that I sank into Abba's enveloping Presence. This enveloping occurred throughout the night.

I want to clarify the point that while Jesus and Abba are separate persons of the God Head, they are one in El Elyon, God Most High.

While it may seem impossible to become one with El Elyon, God Most High, John 17:21 confirms that God does wants us to be one with Him. Jesus stated in that scripture, *that they all may be one, as You, Father, are in Me, and I in You; that they also may be one in Us.*

I experienced a oneness with Jesus in the fall of 2009. Sandra, my wife, awakened me with her coughing. I sat up on the edge of the bed trying to get my bearings. A voice spoke to me saying, "Some doctor you will be you do not have anything in the house to help your wife!" I knew it was the voice of the enemy, for he always finds fault and condemns. I stood up and walked to Sandra's side of the bed. There I placed my right hand on her forehead and left hand on her chest. I began to pray for her healing. In a short while Sandra's coughing ceased, and she went into a deep sleep. Suddenly I was out of my body, standing in the bathroom looking at my body. I saw Jesus' back. He was standing in my body with His right hand on Sandra's forehead and left hand on her chest. His hair was long and dark brown. He wore a white robe. Just as suddenly, I was back in my body with my right hand on Sandra's forehead and left hand on her chest. Jesus spoke to me saying, "You will do this for sick fathers so they can go back to work, sick mothers so they can care for their children, doctors, nurses, mayors, city council members, elected officials, law enforcement personnel, emergency management personnel. There will be many whom you shall touch with the healing power of my love."

This fifth maturity level can be defined as grace. Grace is a person. His name is Jesus. Grace is undeserved, unmerited, and unearned. It is the gift of God through Jesus Christ. As believers in Jesus, we are highly favored (Luke 1:28), greatly blessed (Philippians 4:19), and deeply loved (Romans 5:5).

While reading these five maturity levels, each reader will make a decision as to which level they may be in currently. I pray that should you be in one of the first four maturity levels, you will seek Abba's help to grow the maturity of your spirit heart to the fifth level. Upon finding that you are at the fifth level, be at home there, rejoicing in all that Abba has done for you. Remain there at home with Him for the remainder of your life on this earth. Say as Joshua said, *As for me and my house, we will serve the LORD* (Joshua 24:15).

In Chapters 4 through 6, I will identify three Spirit Life Vital Signs, which are Born of the Spirit, Spiritual Insight, and Right Believing.

I pray that you will continue this journey with me.

Jesus answered, "Most assuredly, I say to you, unless one is born of water and the Spirit, he cannot enter the kingdom of God."
John 3:5

CHAPTER 4: Spirit Life Vital Sign 1–Born of the Spirit

The human body is born of water, which is the amniotic fluid that drains from the amniotic cavity upon rupture prior to birth.[28]

In John 3:5, we read an account of Nicodemus, a Pharisee, member of the Sanhedrin, and renowned master-teacher in Israel, who asked Jesus about being born again.

Jesus replied explaining that a person is born of water and the Spirit. Jesus was explaining that born of water is born of the flesh and is flesh. Water is an amniotic fluid. A baby is born of the flesh which comes from the father and mother through the sperm and ovum, respectively. Throughout the baby's entire development, he is flesh, a human being.

Born of the Spirit is being born again by the sacrificial work performed by Jesus through His death on the cross, burial in a tomb, and resurrection from death to ascend to God the Father from which He came as accounted in John 3:1–13.

When a baby takes his first breath his spirit, the inner man, enters his body. From where does the spirit come? Jeremiah 1:5 states that God knew you before you were formed in your mother's womb. God is all-knowing. He is cognizant of His creation, including mankind. How God knows us before we are formed in our mother's womb is to be taken on faith. There are no scientific studies or reference documents that provide detailed knowledge. However, Psalm 139 gives *God's perfect knowledge of man.*

We learn from verses 1–6 that God knows when we sit down and rise up. He understands our thoughts and knows where we will go and when we will lie down because He is acquainted with all our ways. God knows the words we will speak before they are spoken. He knows us altogether and such knowledge is too wonderful for us to understand. But we can be comfortable with His knowledge of us when we consider that His thoughts are higher than ours and His ways are better than ours.

God reveals greatness to us in verses 7–12 stating that wherever we go He is there, and He always knows where we are regardless of where we go. We cannot hide in the darkness because it is the same to Him as light.

Through verses 13–16 God desires for us to know and accept on faith that He formed our inward parts and covered us in our mother's womb. He sees each of us as being fearfully and wonderfully made. Our bodies are not hidden from God in the

79

womb where we are formed through His procreation process. His eyes saw us even before we were formed in our mother's womb. God remembers each baby whether they are aborted, born prematurely or at full-term, die early due to sickness or accident, or live to an old age because each one is written in His book, and there is a special purpose for each one.

To be clear about what is formed in the womb, it is a physical human body conceived by the father's sperm penetrating the mother's ovum,[29] which is the procreative process God designed and placed into action through Adam and Eve (Genesis 4:1).

God further states in Jeremiah 1:5 that He sanctified you, which means He set you apart for a special purpose.

The special purpose for which you were born of water cannot be activated until you are born of the Spirit. That is because the first man, Adam, disobeyed God's instruction to not eat of the Tree of the Knowledge of Good and Evil. When Adam ate the fruit of that tree, sin entered into all mankind. Jesus came to pay the price for that sin.

While the price has been paid, by Jesus' death, each person must choose Jesus as their Redeemer for their sin-filled spirit or reject Him. When the person receives Jesus as their Redeemer and Savior, they become a new creation in Him

(2 Corinthians 5:17). The old sin-filled spirit is removed, and a new spirit enters the person. The person's spirit is infused with Jesus' life. The new spirit becomes empowered with Jesus' power. The person's life is elevated from a natural plane to supernatural as he or she depends upon Jesus. 1 John 5:4 tells us that whoever is born of God will overcome the world. The victory a born-again believer has for overcoming the world is their faith.

Desiring and receiving salvation by accepting Jesus as our Redeemer, Savior, and Lord, is the first step in allowing God to use us for the special purpose He has called us.

As a thirteen-year-old boy, in 1952, I stepped out of the brown stone duplex house where I lived with my mother. Standing at the edge of the porch, I said, "God, I do not know why I was born. I do not know my purpose in this life. I know that I do not want to be the president of this country or a minister because both of those are criticized a lot."

The remaining years of my childhood passed without hearing from God about the purpose of my life. Yet, somehow, I knew God had his hand on me and was guiding me. I worked different jobs. In between them, I enrolled in college night school. Those years exposed me to many challenges and exciting learning experiences. A valuable lesson I learned through those challenges was that God never failed me and that He would never fail me.

In two different jobs I was introduced to mathematical statistics at an elementary level. As an accounting clerk for the Aluminum Company of American, in New Kensington, PA, in 1962, I was assigned to the Albron Division. That division atomized large aluminum ingots into aluminum powder. The powder was dropped into carts on wheels and manually pushed to shaking screens for separation into powder particle size. The superintendent of the division asked me to determine if using an airveyor to transport the atomized powder to the shaking screens would be cost-effective. First, I had to determine the tare weight of the cart, then the full weight of the cart with the aluminum powder at the atomizing furnace. Second, the weight of the cart with the aluminum powder was determined at the shaking screen before the cart was emptied. The difference between the weight at the atomizing furnace and at the shaking screen represented aluminum powder loss. The total aluminum powder lost per day and working month was given to the superintendent. There was enough loss to justify the purchase and installation of an airveyor.

In 1964, I began working as a cost accountant for the Kelly-Springfield Tire Company in Cumberland, Maryland. Two years later, I took a position of third-shift supervisor in the Stock Preparation Department. The employees on the third-shift had difficulty completing their production schedules due to torn and damaged cloth liners that separated the rubber coated ply stock as it was being rolled.

After talking with the shift foreman and not getting help, I talked with the department manager, but did not get help. I began to count the number of cloth liner rolls that were torn or damaged, thereby making them unavailable to use in production. The count was over 200 on my shift.

The plant manager scheduled a meeting once per month for all supervisors to attend. It began at 8 a.m. Instead of going home I went to the meeting armed with my count of torn and damaged cloth liners. After the plant manager gave an update on production and business results, he asked the attendees if they had any questions. I raised my hand and was recognized to have the floor. Upon standing, I gave my name, shift and department where I worked. In the time given to me, I talked about the inability to meet production schedules due to torn and damaged cloth liners. Then I gave the count of those liners. The plant manager thanked me, and I returned to my seat.

That night when I returned to begin my shift at 11 p.m., there was a written message for me in the Day-Night book in the shift foreman's office. The note was from the division superintendent requesting me to meet with him in his office before I left the plant. At 8 a.m. I was in the division superintendent's office. He thanked me for providing the count of the torn and damaged cloth liners. Then he asked if I had shared that information with the shift foreman and department manager. I said that I did, but no help came. The division superintendent told me that an employee would be on the third-shift the next night to make new cloth liners and repair the torn and damaged ones. Those new and repaired cloth liners were delivered to my stock ply cutting area resulting in meeting production schedules.

On an elementary level I saw how powerful statistics could be in making profitable improvements. The division superintendent talked to me a few weeks later to ask if I would consider relocating to Fayetteville, North Carolina and help with the new plant startup. I relocated to the new plant in 1970 where I became shift foreman of Stock Preparation and Bead Building. In one year, I became the plant superintendent on second-shift.

In addition, I enrolled in a community college to study mathematical statistics at night. A retired Air Force Lieutenant Colonel was my instructor. The best part was that he lived three houses down the street from me. He invited me to his home for private tutoring lessons. I was hooked. Statistics became my career love.

In 1974, I was in Tyler, Texas at a Goodyear Tire & Rubber plant conducting a statistical study on a ten-inch tuber that was used to extrude tire treads. The production manager of the plant, Lowell Hoyt, invited me to eat dinner with him and his wife at their home. After dinner, Lowell and I retired, at his invitation, to his study. There we talked about the statistical study I was conducting. Lowell was extremely interested in how the collection and analysis of data can improve the product. After a thirty-minute discussion, he asked me if I discussed spiritual concepts. I told him of my experience at age eighteen in going to the altar at a church service to receive Jesus. He asked me what my experience had been through the years since age eighteen regarding my walk with Jesus. At the time of our discussion, I was thirty-five years old. Seventeen years had passed, and I could not recount anything significant regarding my walk with Jesus. Then Lowell held out a pen to me and asked, "Do you have this pen?" I smiled and said, "No!" He asked me what I had to do to get the pen.

I replied, "I have to stand up, walk to you and take the pen from your hand." Then Lowell said, "If you want a walk with Jesus, you have to take hold of Him." We talked for another thirty minutes before Lowell drove me to the Ramada Inn where I was staying. I thanked him for the dinner and conversation, then turned and walked into the hotel lobby. My room was at the top of the stairs to the left. After entering the room and closing the door, I dropped to my knees and said, "God, no more deals. No ten percent for You and ninety percent for me. No ninety percent for You and ten percent for me. I want You to have one hundred and ten percent, and if I do not wake up in the morning that will be all right too." That night, I enjoyed the best sleep I ever had. When I awoke, it was the most glorious morning I had ever experienced. Now life was new and exciting!! Upon arrival at the plant, the first person I saw in the office was Lowell. I told him what I had done before going to bed. He could see how excited I was and became excited with me.

Being born again is the first vital sign of a spirit life. It is equivalent to the heart, arteries, vessels, and blood being formed in the human body in the first twelve weeks of life.

Receiving Jesus as Redeemer, Savior, and Lord is like giving a person new life through a heart transplant. Before the transplant, the prognosis is death. After the transplant, the prognosis is to live a long life and fulfill the special purpose God has called you to live.

At the end of July 2007, after my first wife died, Abba Father spoke to me saying, "I wanted you to marry and take care of Nancy, for I knew she would need you the most in her last five years." This knowledge from Abba helped me to understand why, at age seventeen, He told me to marry Nancy.

In May 2008, at the age of sixty-eight and the day after my second wife died, Abba Father showed me Psalm 71:18, *Now also when I am old and gray-headed, O God, do not forsake me, until I declare Your strength to this generation, Your power to everyone who is to come.* I did not know how I was going to declare God's strength to the generation that was living around me, nor did I know how I would declare His power to people not yet alive.

What I did know was that God would make a way for me to declare His strength and power.

In June 2008, while I was attending an Andrew Wommack Gospel Truth Seminar in Duluth, Georgia, Abba told me to attend Charis Bible

College. I spent five hours debating this calling because I had already graduated from various colleges with the last being a doctorate degree.

In my discussion with Abba, I told Him I had an addition to a house that needed to be finished. He replied, "You will get it done." Then I named more projects that needed my attention. After each one, Abba replied, "You will get it done." When I said that I did not know where the Charis Bible College was located and where I would live, He was silent. By the end of the day, I told Abba that I would go to Charis Bible College.

The next day after the seminar closed, I went to the Charis Bible College exhibit. There I learned that a campus existed in Dunwoody, Georgia. Classes would be held Monday to Thursday with a 1 p.m. closing on Thursday. With that information I knew why Abba told me that I would get the projects finished.

On Thursday after class ended, I drove to Mosheim, Tennessee and spent the weekend working on the house addition and other projects while returning to my Dunwoody, Georgia apartment on Sunday to resume classes on Monday.

In May 2010, I graduated as a minister. Remember my talk with God when I was a thirteen-year-old boy? At that time, I did not want to be a minister out of fear of criticism. Along the path of my life, Abba has taught me how to manage criticism. He does not remove those challenges, but He prepares us to manage them fearlessly.

That the God of our
Lord Jesus Christ, the
Father of glory, may give
to you the spirit of
wisdom and revelation in
the knowledge of Him,
the eyes of your
understanding being
enlightened; that you
may know what is the
hope of His calling.

Ephesians 1:17-18

CHAPTER 5: Spirit Life Vital Sign 2--Spiritual Insight

This vital sign of spirit life brings renewing and refreshing to our inner man. It is reminiscent of Psalm 23:2 wherein we are to *lie down in green pastures and be led by the still waters*. That is such a refreshing and renewing thought. It is like breathing fresh crisp air on a mountain top as one takes in the scenery of evergreen trees yielding their balsam fragrance against a snow-capped mountain in the distance.

The Apostle Paul explains in Romans 12:2 that we are to renew our minds. How is such renewing accomplished? It is by hearing, reading, and meditating on God's word. When we do that, the eyes of our heart are opened to spiritual insights that our physical eyes cannot see.

As a first-year student at Charis Bible College-Atlanta, in 2008, I drove home to Mosheim, Tennessee every Thursday afternoon. The drive was on US 23 through Tallulah Falls and Clayton, Georgia to Franklin, North Carolina connecting with Interstate 40 at Waynesville, North Carolina. Then onto Newport, Tennessee arriving at Pates Hill Road, Mosheim, Tennessee. As I drove back to school one Sunday afternoon, I spoke aloud to God, as I drove through Clayton, Georgia, saying, "I do not know why I am going to bible college. I do not want to pastor a church." God replied immediately telling me to go to medical school and gave me a vision of being in the home of a family living in the Appalachian mountains. I was ministering to their health and telling them about Jesus.

In June 2010, I enrolled at Lincoln Memorial University in Harrogate, Tennessee to study pre-med biology with the intention of entering medical school. For three years I went to class but never made it to medical school because of a dream I had on December 2, 2012.

In that dream, I saw myself in an institution, a large building, where I was doing class work. I saw myself working in my home office studying in a variety of ways trying to get the subject matter into my memory. This was a struggle of my own effort instead of total reliance upon God to put the teaching of the material into my memory. I saw that I had to come to the end of myself in doing, through my own efforts, what God asks me to do. I was told that the work was finished, and I was to make a telephone call to let someone in authority know that I was leaving. In the dream, I saw the number 20, which means tried and approved. While the dream surprised me because I thought I was to complete the journey through medical school, I pondered it.

A few years later, God revealed the following to me as His reasons for sending me to Lincoln Memorial University.

I was studying science subjects that He would use through me in the future to help other people. He introduced me to an extremely uncomfortable and difficult situation which was being in classes with eighteen to twenty-two year old students when I was seventy-one years of age. In that environment I learned how to patiently manage mental stress.

He taught me to ask for and trust the Holy Spirit for answers to questions I was not sure about. While the Holy Spirit gave me answers, I did not always rely upon those answers. I would think the correct answer was something else and chose it only to find I was wrong. Once I told the Holy Spirit that I would go with His answer, then a voice came to my mind saying, "What if it is the wrong answer?" I knew that thought came from Satan and replied aloud, if the answer is wrong that is the Holy Spirit's problem. I had come to the point where I knew the Holy Spirit's answer would not be wrong.

God placed me in a rural area that was one and a half hour drive from good restaurants, shops, and quality entertainment so I would not be distracted often by the world's pleasures.

At this point, we are embarking upon a journey. Along the way, we will encounter four mile markers. The fourth is our destination. The first three are preparation for the fourth. I pray that this journey will be both encouraging and educational.

Mile Marker 1: Hearing

We are to take heed, to pay attention to what we hear (Mark 4:24 and Proverbs 4:20–24) because we are to listen for excellent words to be spoken (Proverbs 8:6). Those words may be good advice or excellent counsel. We are to be swift to hear, slow to speak, and slow to wrath (James 1:19). Such swiftness and slowness allow us to pay attention to what is being stated. Thus, those who have ears to hear, will hear (Matthews 11:15). It is like planting good seed in good ground. Those who hear with a noble and good heart keep good advice and excellent counsel, and it bears fruit with patience (Luke 8:15).

On Tuesday, December 17, 2013, the Holy Spirit spoke to my mind, reminding me that I had spent time during the day on Monday, December 16, 2013, pursuing knowledge about naturopathic and homeopathic medicines. He showed me that I was on the wrong path. Instead of putting time into that knowledge, I should be putting my time into strengthening my faith through the studying and understanding of God's word. It is God's word that heals in all situations. God's arm is not short in any situation that requires healing, nor is it short in providing anything we need. I saw that my faith was weak. I also saw that I could not strengthen my faith. It is only the Holy Spirit who can strengthen my faith. However, I must place myself and my mind in a learning environment in which the Holy Spirit can strengthen my faith. I repented while lying in bed and thought that in the morning I will start reading the healing scriptures and like a naughty student, write one hundred times, "I shall study God's word for healing rather than allopathic drugs, naturopathic, or homeopathic medicines." Of course, God does not punish. He only gives loving counsel. The Holy Spirit reminded me that I told one ministry patient to pray before taking the drugs prescribed by her doctor to prevent any adverse reactions in her body. Yet, I had been searching for naturopathic and homeopathic medicines to replace those drugs. Where is the faith in that effort? It is a weak faith! A strong faith would be standing in belief that prayer protects the person's body from any adverse reaction caused by the drugs. Such a belief and prayer helped the person meet her parents' requirements to take the medicine and meet her desire to not be impacted by the side effects of the drugs. I know from this experience that God wants me to allow Him to put His gift of healing and gift of faith into me. I have asked Him for those two gifts. It really is God's work to do in me so He can do His work through me.

If we are to renew and refresh our mind, we do it by faith, which comes by hearing, and hearing by the word of God (Romans 10:17). Jesus said, *My sheep hear My voice, and I know them, and they follow Me* (John 10:27). When we hear in our spirit heart, Jesus calling us to accept Him as our Redeemer, Savior, and Lord, we should listen to His voice, and not harden our spirit heart refusing to receive Him (Hebrews 3:7).

In March 2016, I volunteered to work with the Convention of States Action grassroots organization. I was given a position of District Captain for the Georgia State House district in which I lived. During that month, I talked to other people and made presentations to recruit volunteers. A person called me to inquire about the organization. As I talked to him about becoming a district captain for the district in which he lived, I could tell that he was hesitant to do so. He stated that in checking out the organization, he learned that the state director was a high school student. He was concerned about being in a grassroots organization led by a teenager. I told him how that teenager contributed to the effort that resulted in the Georgia State House of Representatives and State Senate passing legislation in favor of working with the organization to hold a U.S. Constitution Article V convention of states for the purpose of writing amendments to the U.S. Constitution. I also told him that she would graduate from high school that year and a new state director would be placed in her vacancy. As I spoke those words God spoke to my mind saying I would be the new state director. On April 20, 2016, the outgoing Georgia state director called me and asked if I would accept the State Director position. I accept the position knowing that God had given it to me.

Our ears may hear a word behind us, saying, "This is the way, walk in it," (Isaiah 30:21). We should answer that voice with a hearing of faith, allowing our mind to be renewed and refreshed.

I heard a voice speaking to my mind while sitting on the balcony of a church with my wife and children. It was 1975, and I had begun a new position with a new company. There were many issues coming to me at the same time, but I made it through the week. The voice speaking to me said, "Homer, I have been here all week. You only needed to turn around, and you would have received my help." In my mind, I turned and saw Jesus standing in a white garment smiling at me with His arms extended toward me. I was exceedingly small, and He very tall. No longer did I hear the minister's words or see the church's interior. A vision had entered my mind. I saw a slowly curving path ascending a hill. On the left was a wooden rail fence, trees with leaves and fruit, lush green grass, and the air was refreshing.

The entire environment of the scene refreshed me. As the vision faded, I knew that the coming week would be much better.

I answered Jesus' voice with a hearing of faith allowing His peace to renew and refresh my mind.

On January 20, 2021, I shared the following Friday Blessing with those on the list to receive it. The message was from Abba and relates to hearing a whispered voice.

"Be Still . . .
Morning begins slowly quietly with the sun spreading its golden rays bountifully over the mountain tops painting the sky with the power of God's glory. A whispered voice says, 'Be still and know that I am God.' Selah

Suddenly, the air is filled with the sounds of explosions and chaos is fighting to be free. The earth seems to shake, and darkness tries to cover you. The whispered voice is heard again, 'Be still and know that I am God.' Selah

Your attention flees to the voice, and a deep abiding peace washes over you enveloping you. This voice says, 'My child, my friend, be blessed in the protective stillness of the Lord today.' Psalm 46:10."

What are we to do with what we hear? We are to live by those words. We are to put into action what we have heard or read in God's word. His word will change our life. Those changes will be seen by people who know us and those who do not. The actions others see coming from us will carry more weight, have a greater influence, and last longer than any words we speak. We should make our byword or motto, "Live God's word; not my word."

Mile Marker 2: Reading

People read books, articles, documents, or papers for varied reasons—some to establish a career, earn an income, learn a trade, or for pleasure. Most of what people read are for worldly reasons. It is to earn bread. Jesus made a profound statement when He faced Satan in the wilderness. It is recorded in Matthew 4:4 that Jesus answered and said, *it is written, man shall not live by bread alone, but by every word that proceeds from the mouth of God.*

What did Jesus mean? He wants us to open our understanding so that we might comprehend the scriptures (Luke 24:45). Abba Father wants us to know that *whatever things were written before were written for our learning, that we through the patience and comfort of the Scriptures might have hope* (Romans 15:4). He wants us to accept that *all scripture is given by inspiration of God, and is profitable for doctrine, for reproof, for correction, for instruction in righteousness, that the man of God may be complete, thoroughly equipped for every good work* (2 Timothy 3:16–17).

We are to *let the word of God dwell in us richly* (Colossians 3:16), to hide His word in our heart so that we might not sin against Him (Psalm 119:11), and to allow His word to be a lamp to our feet and a light to our path so we do not stumble through this life (Psalm 119:105).

How do we hide God's word in our heart? First, we must sit quietly with Abba so He can build a relationship with us. Abba wants to be our friend and we be His. We find recorded in 2 Chronicles 20:7, that God gave land to the descendants of Abraham, who is His friend forever. Isaiah 41:8, reveals that Abraham is God's friend. Also, James 2:23, states that Abraham was called the friend of God. In fact, Jesus said to His disciplines, as recorded in John 15:13–15, *Greater love has no one than this, than to lay down one's life for his friends. You are my friends if you do whatever I command (instruct) you.* The friendship Abba gives is practical, full of common sense and overflowing with His heavenly Glory.

Abba desires to clear the ashes of loss, hardships, disappointments, and grief from our spirit heart. Then He restores our spirit heart with the oil of joy and a garment of praise (Isaiah 61:3). He wants us to live in His Presence daily. That Presence is Jesus. We are to learn to live on this planet earth, in this physical life, while dwelling in the unseen eternal realm. While living in the Presence of Jesus, we listen and read His word, write notes or thoughts about what we have heard or read. Then we are to take time to meditate, chewing on the word in our thoughts seeking to get the most nourishment and refreshment possible. Looking at our life, we visualize the practical application of what we have heard or read.

On February 12, 2014, Nan*[30], age thirty, called to request prayer for healing. I asked her to describe what was occurring. She gave me a verbal account of the medical report she had received concerning her bodily conditions. I asked her to image my hand touching the top of her head. Then I prayed the peace of Jesus over her mind, nerves, body organs, cells, and her entire being from the top of her head to the bottom of her feet. I explained to her that the medical report was true based on medical statistics and information gathered by the doctor and associated professionals through examinations. However, in the spiritual realm, her conditions are a lie, and the devil is the one who has established the lie in her. In the time of our conversation, I explained that she should no longer read the medical reports or talk to her family members and those outside the family about the report and the conditions she felt in her body. When asked by someone how she was doing she should respond, "By the stripes of Jesus, I am healed." I encouraged her to speak God's word over herself for it is when we confess His word with our mouth that it does not return void to Him. Further, that she should believe and receive that she is healed and what she says and asks God for will be given to her. This young woman had lived under stress for awfully long periods of time. Nan's childhood was filled with rejection and lack of love. She was carrying condemnation deep within her, and that had caused chronic stress, fear, guilt, and confusion. I explained to her that God is not and has never been angry with her because of anything that she may have spoken or did that was deemed wrong. I reminded her that as a born-again believer she is forgiven of all past, present, and future sins and wrong doing, and that she is righteous in God through Jesus Christ. Then I explained that her first action toward healing is to forgive all people who have wronged her and to forgive herself. Then, I told her how the power of her mind will impact her body for good or bad according to her thoughts. Further, I explained how the cells and organs of her body will line up with the mind to punish the body because of guilt and fear resulting from self-condemnation. The devil uses our negative words and actions as opportunities to bring condemnation and fear to influence our mind and bring punishment into our body. Continually speaking about the bad conditions of our body worsens those conditions. However, speaking God's word brings healing to the conditions of our body. I explained that her words are either life or death and that she will eat the fruit of her words.

On February 13, 2014, Nan called from a hospital emergency room to say she had been vomiting and had diarrhea all day. She stated that she thought her stomach was ulcerated. I asked her to place her hand on her stomach and image that my hand was on hers. I prayed that the ulcers were gone from her stomach. Then I expanded the prayer of faith for healing to include her mouth, esophagus, stomach, small intestines, colon, and rectum. I asked Nan to move her hand to her intestines and prayed the prayer of faith that the cells in the intestines become new, for good flora bacteria to enter her intestines, and the diarrhea to stop. Then I prayed Jesus' peace over Nan and told her to rest and not let her heart be troubled or afraid.

On February 14, 2014, Nan called from her room in the hospital to say that her enzymes, fluids, and levels had returned to normal except for sodium, which was only three points low. Her voice was strong, bright, and said that she had eaten a solid breakfast meal. Then Nan said that she and her husband were going to have a steak dinner for their evening meal. Further, Nan said the doctor told her that her quick recovery was a miracle. She told me that she had given her testimony to other medical staff who were suffering from similar illnesses. I rejoiced with Nan and gave her Isaiah 41:10, 13 and 1 Peter 3:7 for her husband so he could provide scriptural support when the enemy (devil) came to torment her for standing against his work on her body. I closed our talk, stating that her faith in Abba to bring healing has made her whole.

God's word will teach and help us to be patient; deal with fear, despair, mental and physical stress; and show us how to manage emotional situations.

As we practice, apply, implement, and work using God's word as our instruction, we will hide His word in our heart. This is experiential learning, which is significantly better than strict memorization.

For newly born-again believers, Abba has provided His Word as pure milk that they may grow (1 Peter 2:2). Hebrews 5:13 confirms that new born-again believers need milk and not solid food, for its states, *you have come to need milk and not solid fool. For everyone who partakes only of milk is unskilled in the word of righteousness, for he is a babe.*

This raises a question about the benefit of a mother's milk for her baby. A mother's breast milk contains antibodies that helps her baby fight off viruses and bacteria. Breastfeeding also lowers a baby's risk of having asthma or allergies. In addition, babies who are breastfed exclusively for the first six months, without any formula, have fewer ear infections, respiratory illnesses, and bouts of diarrhea.[31]

All believers in Jesus have God's protection against terrors, pestilence, plagues, attacks, and destructions (Psalm 91:5-6). For mature born-again believers, Abba's word is solid food that provides guidance for being diligent to present themselves approved to Him, and encouraging a worker not to be ashamed, for rightly dividing the word of truth (2 Timothy 2:15). Hebrews 5:14 confirms that mature believers need the solid food of God's word, for it states, *But solid food belongs to those who are of full age, that is, those who by reason of use have their senses exercised to discern both good and evil.*

.

Mile Marker 3: Meditating

There is an extraordinarily rich word in the Hebrew language for meditate. It is "Hagah," which means "to mutter."[32] When muttering, we are speaking in a low audible voice. In essence, we are talking to ourselves.

The richness of "Hagah" rests in its strength through muttering, which may be thought to be lowly and insignificant. But God loves to use the lowly and insignificant things to shame the things of this world that are displayed to be wise and mighty (1 Corinthians 1:27).

So, how does muttering work? Good question! Let us begin with Psalm 119:15. In that scripture, we are directed to meditate on God's precepts and contemplate His ways. We are to talk to ourselves about a guiding principle we heard or read in God's word as we practice self-control regarding an action we desire not to take or to take one that we desire. Self-control is a fruit of the Holy Spirit: therefore, in our practice of self-control, we meditate, in Abba's presence, seeking His help to not take an action or His way to take an action.

Various scriptures in the Psalms speak of the psalmist loving God's law and meditating on His law (Psalm 1:2, Psalm 119:97). The Hebrew word for law is "Tora," which means "instruction" or "direction."[33] Therefore, we are not meditating on a law that outlines rules. Rules are impersonal. When we mutter, someone hears us. We have a relationship with Abba through Jesus. This relationship brings a personal touch to our muttering. We are to mutter, talk to ourselves, about an instruction or direction Abba has given to us through a dream, vision, or specific word from a scripture in the Bible.

So, what is God's purpose for meditating on His instruction or direction? We find an answer in Job 22:22, which states, *Receive, please, instruction from my mouth, and lay up His words in your heart.*

Laying up God's word in our heart is the operative phrase. Why should we lay up God's word in our heart? Psalm 37:31 answers that question, telling us that by mediating on God's instruction our steps shall not slide or stumble. Therefore, we will walk on a sound foundation. In fact, according to Psalm 119:99, by meditating on God's instruction, we will *have more understanding than all of our teachers.* Now, do not allow that blessing to make you proud, for the *proud will be ashamed* Proverbs 11:2. We are to meditate on God's guiding principles without pride.

When God spoke to Joshua, He instructed him to meditate on the Book of the Law day and night. Was the Book of the Law a list of what to do and not do? No, the Book of the Law are scriptures written by Moses beginning with Genesis and ending with Deuteronomy (Joshua 1:1–9). God wanted Joshua to remember the history of the Hebrew people so they could understand their present days and know what the future would hold for them. Such knowledge could be used by him in leading the nation into the land promised by God.

Today, through meditation on God's word, we can state, as did the psalmist in Psalm 40:8, *I delight to do Your will, O my God, and Your law is within my heart.* When we reach this level of relationship with Abba, and encounter a sleepless night, we can meditate on God's word (Psalm 119:148). When we meditate on God's word during a sleepless night, His promise from Psalm 4:8, *I will both lie down in peace, and sleep*, will be fulfilled. This promise is confirmed in Proverbs 3:24, *When you lie down, you will not be afraid; yes, you will lie down, and your sleep will be sweet.*

Mile Marker 4: Seeing

Our journey through hearing, reading, and meditating has reached seeing. We have arrived at the destination of Spirit Life Vital Sign 2, which is Spiritual Insight.

On this journey, there were glimpses of a spirit life relationship with God's word. Those glimpses may have been encouraging or not. I pray that the journey was thought-provoking. The intent of the previous mile markers is to open spiritual eyes, which are the eyes of the spirit heart. Prior to being born-again, our spirit dwelled in a rebellious house called the world. In that house, we had eyes to see but could not see, and ears to hear but could not hear (Ezekiel 12:2).

In that rebellious house, we were one of many foolish people without an understanding of God's ways. Our natural eyes could not see God's ways, nor our natural ears hear His voice (Jeremiah 5:21). We were like the men with Daniel when he saw a vision from God. Those men *did not see the vision, and a great terror fell upon them, so that they fled to hide themselves* (Daniel 10:7). And the men who travelled with Saul, who became the Apostle Paul, *stood speechless when the light of Jesus came upon Saul. They heard a voice but did not see anyone* (Acts 9:7).

With our natural eyes and ears, *none of the things from God could enter our heart; things He had prepared for those who love Him* (1 Corinthians 2:9).

The message of the previous mile markers may have revealed spiritual insight dimly. The goal of seeing is to see Abba face to face in His word and the dreams and visions He gives.

Earlier in this book I talked about my wife Sandra wakening me with loud coughing. It was when I placed my right hand on her forehead and my left on her chest praying for the bronchitis to leave that I saw Jesus standing in my body with His back to me. His right hand was on Sandra's forehead and His left on her chest. Since having this vision of Jesus, I have had many occasions to pray healing over people. Some have experienced healing. Some have not and died.

On December 7, 2012, I had a vision in which the American Medical Association brought a lawsuit against me for practicing medicine without a license or medical board certification. I was not nor am I a degreed medical doctor. A part of Love Life Ministry is praying with people for healing of their sickness or difficult life issues. In this vision, I was sitting with my attorney, listening to the prosecution speak and watching the judge. The judge was having a difficult time concentrating on what was being said and the documents he had in front of him. I spoke to my attorney, saying, "Ask the judge for a brief recess in his chambers with you, me and the prosecuting attorney." My attorney looked at me as if to ask why. I asked my attorney if my request was out of order. He replied that it was not. Then I told him to do it for the Holy Spirit is leading me to request the recess.

The request was granted, and the prosecuting attorney, my attorney, and I retired to the judge's chambers with him. In the chamber, the judge asked me what the recess was about. I replied, "The Holy Spirit has shown me that you are in pain. Is that correct?" The judge replied that his back was hurting very badly. I asked him if he would allow me to pray for him. He said if I thought it would help, he would allow it. As I placed my hand under his robe, I told the judge to say what he felt as I prayed. Shortly after I began praying against the pain, casting it out in Jesus' name, the judge told me and the two attorneys that he felt a warm soothing sensation going through his back and the pain was going away. I stopped praying when the judge told me that the pain was gone. I stepped back and looked at the judge. He said to me, "I cannot allow what you did for me to influence my decision about the charges brought against you." I replied, "The healing you received is only to restore you so you can concentrate on what you hear from the attorneys and what you read in the documents. With the pain, you cannot function properly." Then we returned to the courtroom.

When the judge returned to his seat, he asked the prosecuting attorney to instruct a specific doctor to take the witness stand for questioning. The judge asked the doctor if he was his (the judges') physician. The doctor replied that he was. The judge asked the doctor if he had been treating him (the judge) for back pain. The doctor replied that he had been. The judge asked the doctor how long he had been treating him. The doctor replied that the back pain had persisted for years, but that it was manageable with prescription drugs. Then the judge said to the doctor, "You have been my physician for many years, and you have treated me for back pain, but you have never been able to remove the pain. Today, in my chambers, Mr. Crothers touched my back and prayed for the pain to leave. I felt the pain leave. I have no pain now. What you could not do through medicine for years, Mr. Crothers did in a few minutes with the power of God. I rule in favor of Mr. Crothers. He is not practicing medicine without a license. This case is dismissed."

As the courtroom was clearing, the judge was rising from his chair behind the bench and he called out, "Mr. Crothers, please come to my chambers." When I entered the judge's chambers, he said to me, "I want to know your God." I asked the judge if Jesus was his Savior and Lord. He replied no to my question. I asked him if he wanted to receive Jesus as his Savior and Lord, to which he replied yes. The judge received Jesus as his Savior and Lord. He was extremely excited about going home to tell his wife all about what had happened to him that day.

We all know how to imagine. We can see, in our mind's eye, the car, boat, house, or vacation we want. What we want most we can even imagine how it will become ours.

For most of our life, the things we imagine are of the physical realm, and the way to get them is also of the physical realm. God is not stingy! He is not trying to keep something from us. He does not set expectations or criteria that must be met before He gives what we ask. God's way is different than our way. He tells us to believe that we have what we want before we receive it.

Did I just hear, "What!!! Believe I have it before I see it or hold it!" You did read correctly. That which we desire to have we are to believe that we have it. Believing brings spiritual insight.

When God told Abraham that he would have an heir, a son, from his body, he believed God

(Genesis 15:4–6). Abraham was shown stars in the heavens and sand on the ground. These helped him to imagine the great nation he would foster through his son of promise.

Isaac, Abraham's son, believed he would receive a crop when he planted during a famine in the land. He planted and reaped a hundredfold (Genesis 26:1–14). Isaac imagined the seed sprouting and growing into plentiful heads of grain. He was given what he imagined.

Jesus told His disciples to have faith in God. When they do, they could tell a mountain to jump into the ocean, if they did not doubt in their hearts. The disciples only had to believe without doubting and say what they wanted to happen (Mark 11:22–24).

What we want, we can have when we believe without doubting in our heart! We can have what we imagine, what we do not see, when we believe.

Jesus used a metaphor to help His disciples understand how they could have what they imagined. He stated in John 15:1 that He was the *true vine* and God, His Father, was the *vinedresser*. Continuing with His teaching, as recorded in John 15:2–8, Jesus' goal was to help the disciples see that when they abided in Him, they would see great success in whatever they did.

First, Jesus wanted the disciples to know that they were the branches who were in Him. If any of the disciples did not bear fruit, the vinedresser, God, would remove them. At this point, it is good to recall that the disciple, Judas Iscariot, denied Jesus by selling His identity and location to the Sanhedrin then leading them to the garden where Jesus was with the other disciples. There Judas kissed Jesus' cheek, which was a signal to the chief priests, scribes, and elders that He was the man to arrest (Mark 14:43–44). Judas, thus, became a branch that did not bear fruit and was removed. The removal began during the Last Supper, when Jesus dipped bread with Judas, he said *Rabbi is it I?* Jesus replied, *you have said it.* (Matthew 26:25). Then Judas went out of the room departing for a meeting with the chief priests and captains to betray Jesus for thirty pieces of silver (Luke 22:3–6, Matthew 26:14). The removal of Judas, as a branch from the vine, was completed by his own act of hanging himself after he realized that he had betrayed an innocent man, who was to die by crucifixion.

Second, part of the teaching revealed that branches bearing fruit were pruned so that they would bear more fruit. Do you see the growth from *bear fruit* to *bear more fruit*?

While a human vinedresser prunes off dead branches by cutting them, they do not cut off branches that are bearing fruit while lying on the ground. The branches on the ground are lifted, cleaned, and reinstated alongside the other branches so they can bear more fruit.

Our Abba Father does the same with His children who have fallen in the world and become lost, confused, soiled, and weak. With one cry from us, Abba reaches down and picks us up. He holds us tenderly while cleaning and clearing away the dirt of the world. After strengthening us, He restores us to Himself so that we can bear more fruit.

Jesus makes an emphasis for which He really wants us to get a good hold. We are to know that without Him we can do nothing enduringly successful. We can do something without Jesus' guidance. I have found that whatever I complete without the Holy Spirit's guidance and help becomes my next problem. Then, I have to call upon Him to help me by cleaning up the mess I made.

At the writing of this book, I installed a paver and field stone walkway with steps. In the last section of the walkway, at the top of the slope, I was in a hurry to complete the project and did not look at the alignment of the pavers. In my rush to complete it, I cut about an inch off of three pavers and installed them. Then I proceed to lock the pavers in place by cementing field stone at the opposite side from the concrete pad that the walkway met. Now that all is dry and firm, I see the misalignment. I have asked the Holy Spirit to show me how to correct my error. He has given me a method. I will follow it because I know that when I do, His solution always works.

We abide in Jesus through the hearing, reading, and meditating on God's word. Continuing to hear, read, and meditate keeps us from becoming a withered branch. We are promised that as we continue to abide in God's word, we can ask whatever we desire, and it shall be done for us (John 15:7). As we continue to abide in God's word, Abba is glorified, and we bear much fruit.

I call your attention to the growth we experience as we hear, read, and meditate on God's word. In John 15:2, we *bear fruit*. John 15:5 tells us we *bear much fruit*. John 15:8 reveals that our continuance in God's word *glorifies Abba, and we bear much fruit*.

There are great advantages in having spiritual insight. In this world, we will see the prosperity of the wicked, their eyes bulging with abundance; nevertheless, we will put our trust in Abba, so that we may declare all His works (Psalm 73). With spiritual insight we will see how Satan, the enemy of all people, has blinded unbelievers so they cannot see the light of the gospel of the glory of Christ, who is the image of God, that it should shine on them (2 Corinthians 4:3–4).

But having the same spirit of faith, according to what is written, "I believed; therefore, I spoke," we also believe; therefore, we also speak.

2 Corinthians 4:13

CHAPTER 6: Spirit Life Vital Sign 3—Right Believing

What is right believing? The word right indicates that there is an opposite. Perhaps it is wrong believing. If one can believe right, then one can also believe wrong. Both "right" and "wrong" require a standard or guideline in order to determine if the action is right or is wrong. A standard has been written, by which we can measure our believing. It is the Holy Bible!

I want to establish the creditability of the standard for right believing. The scripture of 2 Timothy 3:16-17 states, *All Scripture is given by inspiration of God, and is profitable for doctrine, for reproof, for correction, for instruction in righteousness, that the man of God may be complete thoroughly equipped for every good work.*

Walk with me through an explanation of 2 Timothy 3:16–17 so the standard for right believing can be understood.

From this scripture, we see that God inspired men to write His word. God's intention for His word is that we use it as a guide. 1 Thessalonians 2:13 confirm this wherein we learn that when *anyone receives God's word by hearing or reading it is welcomed for it is not the word of men. Rather, it is in truth, the word of God, which works effectively in those who believe it.*

Also, 2 Peter 1:20–21 confirms that *no prophecy of scripture is of any private interpretation. Prophecy never came by the will of man, but by holy men of God who spoke as led by the Holy Spirit.*

Further, 1 Corinthians 2:13 supports what Peter wrote in 2 Peter 1:20–21, *these words we speak, not in words which man's wisdom teaches but which the Holy Spirit teaches, comparing spiritual things with spiritual.*

God's word guides us to see that it is His doctrine. A doctrine can be a principle or a body of principles that are accepted or believed.[34] Titus 1:9 supports this, *holding fast the faithful word as he has been taught, that he may be able, by sound doctrine, both to exhort and convict those who contradict.*

Mature believers are those who are faithful in their acceptance of the entire Holy Bible as the body of principles by which to live.

Looking inside 2 Timothy 3:16–17, we learn that reproof is to reject or disapprove.[35] Therefore, God's word is to be used as proof for something that has been misstated, misrepresented, or something that has been proclaimed as true, when it is false. (2 Timothy 4:2)

It is interesting and shows God's thoroughness, that correction follows reproof in 2 Timothy 3:16.

Correction is the act of making right what has been said or done wrong.[36] Therefore, it is an action that a person must take to change wrong believing to right believing. (2 Timothy 2:25)

I remember a friend telling me he did not like instruction. It was because he rebelled at the instruction of his father. Sadly, that rebellion stayed with the man past his father's death. Proverbs 5:12–13 warns us about instruction saying, *how I hated instruction, and my heart despised correction!* Therefore, it is wise to receive instruction in righteousness in order to understand it. The word "right" as an adjective means to be in accordance with what is just, good, or proper.[37] When I see the words "just" and "good," I think of Micah 6:8, *He has shown you, O man, what is good; and what does the LORD require of you but to do justly, to love mercy, and to walk humbly with your God?*

When "ous" is added to "right" the word becomes an adjective suffix that means full of or abounding in. Therefore, "righteous" means that one is filled with a desire to do whatever needs to be done in accordance with what is just and good.[38]

When "ness" is added to "righteous" the adjective suffix becomes a noun, which we know describes a person, place, or thing. Thus, "righteousness" means state, condition, quality, or degree of the person.[39]

The following message is shared from Joseph Prince Ministries Daily Grace Inspiration dated October 20, 2021, via email to me, the emphasis are mine.

Joseph Prince states, "Your weapons for this warfare are found in the truth of God's word, and they are mighty and have the power to overthrow and destroy every stronghold that has been built up through disinformation and **wrong believing**. And the way we can destroy these strongholds in our mind is by "bringing every thought into captivity to the obedience of Christ" (2 Cor. 10:5).

When I was a young believer, I was taught that it was my responsibility to bring my every thought into obedience **to** Christ. I tried and struggled with that for years and ended up with more mental oppression, stress, and guilt than I had started with.
One day God opened my eyes and said to me, "Son, keep your focus and your thoughts always on the obedience **of Christ**, and that will be a powerful weapon to pull down the devil's strongholds in your mind." When He said that to me, it felt like the lights were suddenly switched on in my head.

So, what does it mean to capture every thought to the obedience of Christ? Simply this: to focus on Jesus' obedience to the Father at the cross, through which we were all made forever righteous the moment we believed in Him.

Can you see that our obedience today under the new covenant begins with choosing to **believe** that we are made righteous by **Christ's obedience** at the cross? The apostle Paul describes our obedience as "obedience to the faith" (Rom. 16:26)—**believing right** about what Jesus has done to make us righteous. And when we **believe right** like this, we will find His grace motivating and empowering us to think and live right. God's word tells us, "The just [righteous] shall live by faith" (Rom. 1:17). You can say it like this: the righteous shall live by **right believing**. When you have **right believing**, you release the power of God to live right.

The next time you have negative thoughts, catch yourself and look toward the obedience of Christ. See the cross. See Jesus. See Him washing your mind with His precious blood.

When you believe the gospel, the true gospel that says you are righteous through Jesus' obedience (Rom. 5:19), you will have **right living**. The right results will follow.

My friend, the more you **believe right** that you have been made righteous and blessed through Christ's obedience, the more you will see the fruit of obedience in your life. Praise Jesus for His marvelous grace!"[40]

Now, we know that "righteousness" describes a person as being full of a desire to do whatever needs to be done in accordance with what is just and good. This should be a lesson from Micah 6:8 for all believers.

I submit that 2 Timothy 3:16–17 establishes a firm foundation for right believing. An example of right believing is recorded in Acts 15:9 where the Apostle Luke writes that the Apostle Peter met with the Jerusalem Council. In that meeting, Peter stated that the hearts of the Gentile believers were purified by faith. Peter was talking about Cornelius, a centurion of the Italian Regiment, who had summoned him to his house because a man in bright clothing appeared before him as he prayed. When Peter arrived, Cornelius and his family and relatives waited to hear what he had to say. While Peter was telling them about Jesus, the Holy Spirit fell upon all of them, and they received salvation. Their salvation did **not come by works, but by** believing right.

Following is a testimony of right believing that I received from Carl*[41], a Christian brother.

"Four days before speaking at a church in Mississippi, my car engine failed. The cost to repair was $4,000, which we did not have. We paid by credit card, believing God would provide. Upon arriving at the church, the pastor gave us a check for $4,000 not knowing about the car engine repair. My wife, Ashley*[42], told the pastor about the failure of their car's engine and how they believed that if they repaired it God would provide the money to pay their repair bill. The pastor praised God for being faithful to Carl and his wife."

2 Corinthians 4:13 tells us that a spirit of faith resides in us. Therefore, we should speak what we believe! Mark 11:22–24 tells us *when we do not doubt but believe that those things we say will be done, we will have whatever we say.*

In Chapter 5 I talked about Nan*[43] a thirty year old female who had contacted us for healing prayer. Nan, at the time of her initial call to us, had Addison's disease, which is a rare but serious adrenal gland disorder.

Addison's disease adversely impacts the production of two critical hormones: cortisol, and aldosterone.[44] Nan had been on hormone replacement therapy medication to provide her body the level of the two hormones needed. According to the American Medical Association, hormone replacement therapy is needed for the remainder of one's life.

One day in March 2014, Nan called to say that the Holy Spirit had led her to discontinue the hormone replacement therapy medication because she was healed. Her hesitation came because her husband was afraid that if she did not take the medicine, she would become sick and be hospitalized. I told Nan that her husband has the responsibility from God to be the spiritual leader of the family. As his wife, she is to follow her husband's guidance. I told her that if her adrenal glands are healed and the correct level of cortisol and aldosterone are being produced, she would experience some sickness when taking the hormone replacement therapy medication because there would be an excess of each in her body.

About three weeks later, Nan called to say that she had become sick and went to the doctor, who evaluated her body for cortisol and aldosterone. The doctor found those hormones to be in excess and discontinued the hormone replacement therapy medication.

Nan experienced healing because of her right believing. Her faith led her to know for certain that the Holy Spirit spoke truth about the healing of her adrenal glands.

While she believed she was healed, she wanted to honor her husband's request to not stop taking the

133

medicine. Abba saw her faith and met it through the healing of her adrenal glands.

James 4:3 teaches that *we do not have because we do not ask, or we ask and do not receive because we ask amiss.*

Fran*[45] was age forty-seven and diagnosed with cancer in her left leg and knee in October 2013. She had taken ten radiation treatments on the left knee and thigh. When my wife and I visited Fran in her home, she was sitting in a wheelchair in a sedated condition. Fran opened her eyes when we began talking, then closed them again. In a short time, Fran awakened and began to talk. She shared that she was afraid she was going to die and that she had seen the spirit of death.

We shared God's word, reminding her that God does not give a spirit of fear. He gives power, love, and a sound mind. The enemy, Satan, brings fear and influences a person to condemn themselves for past mistakes and abusive treatment brought by someone. We further shared the truth of God's word that Jesus had taken all of her sickness and diseases into Himself at the whipping post and on the cross. Fran's own words were spoken to her so she could see how she spoke condemnation to herself. We administered Holy Communion to her demonstrating God's way of giving her assurance that Jesus' healing is in her body. Fran prayed in agreement, rebuking and casting out the spirit of death, spirit of condemnation, and spirit of fear. My eyes were closed in prayer, yet I saw those three evil spirits depart from Fran. We told Fran to continue the medications and treatment that her doctors had prescribed. As we were leaving Fran's house, we assured her that we would return the next day.

Upon arrival at Fran's home the next day, we found her to be alert with a pleasant and happy demeanor. She stated that her night's sleep was the best she had experienced for weeks.

We shared more of God's word about healing with Fran and her son and daughter-in-law. Healing music was played for her. Holy Communion was administered to Fran and her daughter-in-law.

As we departed Fran's home, we told her to continue the medications and treatment prescribed by her doctors. The next day, we answered questions asked by Fran and her husband regarding healing. We were told that the physical therapist had not come for almost a week due to a fracture found in Fran's left leg. We assisted her as she desired to exercise her legs. Sitting on the bed Fran slowly straightened her left leg but was unable to make it completely straight. Then she sat on the edge of her bed and did the leg exercises that the physical therapist had shown her.

Again, healing music was played, and Holy Communion was administered to Fran and her husband. They were encouraged to partake in the Holy Communion at least three times each day. Fran was encouraged to eat protein and carbohydrates to strengthen her body and give her energy.

We read 1 Peter 3:7 for Fran's husband and explained his role in caring for his wife. Then we encouraged him to have some time away from the house doing whatever he enjoyed. Such a time would strengthen and encourage him in his role of caregiver. We talked with Fran about her relationship with her husband and encouraged them to talk about everything and to forgive one another when sharp words and short tempers were evident.

Our visits continued with Fran through the remainder of 2013 and into 2014. We saw cells form in open wounds on her back and breast until they were completely healed. Her spirit was lifted, and emotions were good until April 2014. In that month we brought Fran into our home so we could minister to and provide care over a twenty-four hour period as needed. It appeared that while we were fighting against the enemy, we were losing the battle for Fran because her will to live had lost purpose each day.

An appointment was made for Fran with a doctor who took an x-ray of her left hip. It was then we found that the ball on Fran's hip was out of the sock. We encouraged her to accept an appointment with a surgeon to replace the ball into the sock and secure it. But when Fran saw the black spots on her pelvis bone in the x-ray, she gave up completely. She asked us to take her back to her home. In one month, she died.

Fran had many challenges. During her childhood, she experienced verbal abuses from her father, who threatened to kill her. At that time, Fran was fourteen, which is the age she ran away from home. She was found by law enforcement and returned to her parents. Fran's mother made her stay in the background at church and other places she was taken. She lived with much self-condemnation, fear, and guilt.

Fran was divorced from first husband, who used her in pornographic postures taking her photographs and distributing them. In her second marriage, Fran not only experienced challenges of illness in her body, but she also had challenges from her husband and son who were not making the effort to help her. Instead, they wanted her home so she could cook for them. They did not realize how much Fran had going against her. Sadly, under those conditions, Fran did not believe that she could be healed. None of Fran's illnesses were too hard for God to take away. But God will not force Himself on anyone. He has given us free will. We shall have what we believe and say, therefore, I encourage you to believe that God wants the best for you. Be bold and ask for what you think is impossible, then stand and see God work for you.

Tumultuous times cause us to lose our way and forget the One who knows the way out. During those times, we are to believe that Abba knows the way through tumultuous times, and He will lead us to safety and comfort.

When my children were young, we drove from Tennessee to West Virginia to visit their grandparents, a trip of 500 miles taking ten hours. My daughter, Lori Ann, asked me several times along the way if we were there yet. I knew the way, where we were, and assured her we were almost there. My children relied upon me to know the way and get them safely to their grandparents.

God wants us to rely upon Him, in our tumultuous days, to get us through them. He knows the way and will keep us safe, while providing for us. You are blessed when you believe and trust the Lord, for His ways never fail. He is the abundance of your needs. His perfect love casts out all fear. Look to God, your Father, to walk you through tumultuous times. It is possible to make a journey through life experiencing multiple miracles only to arrive at a point when sickness comes and displaces right believing. The reason right believing can be displaced by sickness is that we allow wrong believing to enter our spirit heart. What we allow into our spirit-heart often becomes overwhelming. Instead, we should speak against any sickness by faith in God because right believing overcomes wrong believing. Such wrong believing can confine a person to a wheelchair unable to walk because there is a great fear of falling and a lack of confidence and faith to try.

Eve *[46] loved the Lord deeply. She believed God had called her to ministry as a pastor. The pastor of her local church believed that Eve was called to pastor a church. Eve's belief turned into an effort of her own to fulfill God's call on her life. Someone can become so obsessed to complete something that they forget God's word in Ephesians 4:1–6. Therein, we are told *to walk worthy of our calling with lowliness and gentleness, with longsuffering and bearing with one another in love endeavoring to keep the unity of the Spirit in the bond of peace.* Eve forced her husband to move from their home state to a new location. Once established in her new location, Eve started a local church. It lasted three years before failing. This occurred three times over a number of years.

When we take a calling out of God's hands, believing we can do it, our efforts will fail. God calls us to walk beside Him allowing Him to do the work. We should remember that God knows everything; therefore, He knows the best way to do something and the best time to do it. All of Eve's efforts and her poor relationship with her domineering mother put a lot of stress on her heart and body. Eve experienced a stroke which put her in a wheelchair for years.

Now, Eve's health and mobility are beginning to improve. She made a decision not to allow her mother to influence her decisions, therefore her life. She has renewed her commitment to God's calling with an attitude to follow His guidance. We may think we are believing right, but when we are experiencing failure after failure, troubled relationships, and poor heath, we should pause and ask God for His help.

An important principle we should learn about right believing is that when we rest God works. Luke 12:32 tells us that *it is our Father's good pleasure to give us the kingdom.* His kingdom begins in this life on this earth.

In his book "The Tongue: A Creative Force" on pages 70-73, Charles Capps says that he had previously been a farmer with 800 acres of land. After he planted cotton, he would say, "Well, it doesn't make any difference how deep I plant it, it will probably rain three inches, and it won't come up anyway." It rained and the cotton did not come up. Charles planted cotton again but to a shallow depth, about a half inch deep, and told everyone, "Now it will turn off dry and won't rain for three weeks." It did just what he said. He planted cotton again and repeated more negative words. Only two-thirds of his cotton crop came up. And Charles said, "Now there will probably come an early freeze and kill it before it opens." That is what happened. Charles farmed those 800 acres for two years while speaking negative words over the crops. He did not make enough money to buy a driver's license. He said, "The farming practices that once worked for me did not work. The same ground that once produced bounteously now refused to respond."[47]

What did Charles do? He still believed the word concerning giving in Luke 6:38 and continued to give. He prayed, repented, and begged God to prosper him, but nothing worked. He was still negative. His confession destroyed his prayer. Then a Baptist man came to Charles' house and brought some books for him. One of those books was *Right and Wrong Thinking* by Kenneth Hagin. Charles read a statement made by Kenneth Hagin

141

in his book that turned Charles' thinking and words around. It was, *People that think wrong believe wrong, and when they believe wrong, they act wrong.* Finally, Charles Capps learned that his negative words resulted in wrong actions and produced wrong results.[48]

Charles Capps wanted other people to learn the lessons he had learned. He soon authored a book, "God's Creative Power® for Healing." In the Introduction of his book on page 4, he states, "Medical science tells us there are many incurable diseases such as some forms of cancer, arthritis, heart disease and AIDS, just to name a few. This book presents supernatural help to all people with incurable diseases. God's word is supernatural. Mixing faith with God's word by speaking it out of your mouth is a means of applying God's medicine. The rest is up to the individual as to whether or not they have the confidence to take God's medicine on a regular basis."[49]

When we do not believe right, our words will be wrong and give us outcomes we do not want.

We were referred to Rae*[50] who was suffering with cancer. When we visited Rae in her home, she had inflammation of the brain, pressure behind her left eye and loss of sight, cancer in her liver and pancreas, pain and swelling in her abdomen, and weakness in her legs. Such a list of major illnesses as this would likely cause anyone to give up hope. The probable cause of Rae's condition was the fact that she lived in a childhood of criticism and without expression of love. We learned from Rae that her father was an alcoholic and that she could not meet her mother's performance expectations. We asked Rae if her mother knew of her illness, to which she said that she had not seen her mother for ten years. Now that she was sick her mother came to visit her and expressed her love by buying bed clothes and other things that were needed. Unfortunately, Rae brought her childhood experience into her marriage and family. As a result, she experienced a divorce more than two years earlier. Rae had given up because her husband gave up on her. We talked with Rae saying that the first step in her healing is to forgive her husband, father, mother, and her two daughters and son. We told Rae that these are the people with whom she had issues and her forgiveness of them and their forgiveness of her would open the door for her healing. We worked with Rae and her son, trying to clear the air of disagreement between them. It appeared that progress had been made.

Rae told us that she was saved, baptized in the Holy Spirit, and spoke in tongues. Yet, we knew that Rae's desire to be healed was weak. We prayed over Rae with her agreement speaking in Jesus' name against cancer in her brain, esophagus,

143

stomach, liver, pancreas, intestines, colon, rectum, lymph nodes and system, all cells, tissue, and muscles. We prayed for strength to enter her legs, for functionality and peace over her entire digestive system, and that the pressure behind her left eye be removed and for full functionality of her ears to become apparent. We prayed the peace of Jesus into Rae's entire body and that she would not let her heart be troubled or afraid.

One week after our visit, the son sent a text stating that his mother had died. This news hurt our hearts because we knew that her healing was just as assured as the woman with the twelve year issue of blood accounted for in Luke 8:43–48. When that woman found her way to Jesus and touched the hem of his robe, she was healed instantly. Jesus turned and told her that it was her faith in Him that healed her.

It is sad to see people who are sick, yet so close to the source of their healing, and cannot cry out to Jesus for the healing He paid for them to have at the whipping post and on the cross. Proverbs 12:18 speaks volumes to me. The first part states, *there is one who speaks like the piercings of a sword*. The enemy's voice brings negative statements to our mind. Those statements when we receive them go into our spirit heart, then we say those words, and they defeat us.

The second part of Proverbs 12:18 states, *but the tongue of the wise promotes health*. Such a tongue should be used by believers in order to keep their body and mind in good health. We must be careful to speak the right words because we possess the power to speak life or death over ourselves. Do you believe this? It is important to believe right.

For another example, I reach back to 1517, where we find the work of Martin Luther, who spent his early years in relative anonymity as a monk and scholar. In his study and research about the contemporary usage of penance and righteousness, he believed that the church did not see the central truths of Christianity, which is the doctrine of justification by faith alone. Therefore, in an attempt to change the wrong belief to right belief, Luther penned a document revealing the Catholic Church's corrupt practice of selling "indulgences" to absolve sin,[51] stating, "This one and firm rock, which we call the doctrine of justification, is the chief article of the whole Christian doctrine, which comprehends the understanding of all godliness."[52] Therefore, Luther accepted that justification is entirely by God's work. He stood against the teaching that believers are made righteous through the Holy Spirit infusing an individual in the sacrament of baptism with both grace and virtue.[53] Rather he taught that righteousness only comes from Christ because it is His righteousness and comes from outside the person. Therefore, it comes from faith. Luther stated[54] That is why faith alone makes someone just and fulfills the law. Faith is that which brings the Holy Spirit through the merits of Christ"[55]

When someone believes right, faith in that belief grasps the believer's heart and they stand firm. Martin Luther is an example of such a person.

Daily, our believing will be challenged. I find that 2 Corinthians 10:5 helps to keep me believing right for it states, *casting down arguments and every high thing that exalts itself against the knowledge of God bringing every thought into captivity to the obedience of Christ.*

I pray that 2 Corinthians 10:5 shall become a word from God that we all speak in times of wrong believing.

For now, we see in a mirror dimly, but then face to face. Now I know in part, but then I shall know just as I also am known.

1 Corinthians 13:12

REFLECTION

This journey we have embarked upon has reached its destination! However, a journey is not complete without some reflection on what has been seen or learned.

At the beginning, the vital signs of the human body were identified as pulse rate, respiratory rate, and body temperature.

Spirit life vital signs have been identified as Born-Again, Spiritual Insight, and Right Believing.

A sign of no pulse rate means the physical heart is not functioning. Without a functioning physical heart, there is no blood flow through the human body. A lack of blood flow results in the death of the body. Finally, without a functioning heart there is no respiratory rate, and the body temperature goes below that which sustains life in the body.

Not being born-again, the first vital sign of the spirit life, means that the spirit is already in a state of death, but the human body is alive and functioning. A dead spirit life is not like a dead physical body. A dead spirit life is living in death. This condition could be likened to the TV series *The Walking Dead* in which the characters are people who survived a zombie apocalypse. [56]

When the spirit life is dead and the physical body dies, the dead spirit life goes to Hell and resides in that place of torment and pain. The worst days of a dead spirit life on earth will be the best days in Hell.

As a functioning physical heart provides life to the physical body, so a born-again spirit allows abundant life to enter the spirit and bring blessings of health and long life to the physical body.

A physical body with a pulse rate also needs a respiratory rate in order to continue life. When the respiratory rate is too low or too high, medical procedures can be implemented in order to stabilize the body. Such procedures ensure that the body will continue to have a flow of oxygen, which is vital.

Likewise, the spirit life vital sign of spiritual insight provides spiritual renewal to the spirit life. The renewal process begins with what our eyes see, and ears hear. That information goes into our mind then into our spirit heart. The spirit life lives out of the spirit heart. Thus, the Apostle Paul wrote in Romans 12:2 that *we should not be conformed to this world but be transformed by the renewing of our mind.*

Such transformation is accomplished by the hearing, reading, and meditating on God's word. This process is like deoxygenated blood traveling to the lungs where a gas exchange takes place, allowing the carbon dioxide in deoxygenated

151

blood to leave the body and fresh oxygen to enter into the blood and be carried throughout the physical body.

Hearing and reading God's word is taking nourishment and healing into our spirit heart. Meditating on what we hear and read in God's word is digesting it for the nourishment, healing and strengthening of our spirit heart.

It was shown, at the beginning of this journey, that body temperature is vital to the continuation of life. When body temperature increases or decreases from the normal range, there are automatic functions that occur. Blood vessels will constrict when the body temperature is too low and dilate when the temperature is too high.

The spirit life vital sign right believing is a controlling function of the spirit life as body temperature is for the physical body. It has been shown that our soul is our mind, will, and emotions. Emotion is an indicator of whether we are believing right or wrong. When we allow our carnal mind, the mind of the flesh, to be in control, our emotions usually go out of control. When we are actively in the carnal mind state, we are believing wrong. Allowing the Mind of Christ to be in control will result in our emotions being in control. In the Mind of Christ state, we are believing right.

Body temperature and emotions have a similar effect on the physical body. The body is cold when its temperature is low and hot when the temperature is high. Emotions can cause our body to be in stress and that condition usually makes the body feel hot but can also make it feel cold. Therefore, when we are actively in the Mind of Christ right believing is occurring. In that state, should events happen that impact our emotions, we are able to remain stable resulting in control of the emotions. Thus, the body is not subject to stress that can cause a fluctuation in body temperature.

The purpose of our journey was to identify vital signs of life in our spirit. We now know those vital signs to be Born-Again, Spiritual Insight, and Right Believing.

It is my hope that you, dear reader, will spend adequate time in God's word alone with Him. Doing so will allow God to become your Abba Father. Spending time in His word and alone with Him will let Him increase your understanding of the vital signs of life in your spirit, and help you practice living in them. This will help you cope with the difficulties of life. See the word "cope" as challenges, obstacles, problems, and errors. How you manage each of those determines who you are trying to please. Giving difficult issues you are trying to cope with to Abba Father allows Him to meet your needs superabundantly. Your solutions for fixing those difficult issues become your next problem.

Reading and meditating on Ephesians 3:20 will help you practice the vital signs of your spirit life: *Now to Him who is able to do exceedingly abundantly above all that we ask or think, according to the power that works in us,* and Colossians 3:23–24 *whatever you do, do it heartily, as to the Lord and not to men, knowing that from the Lord you will receive the reward of the inheritance; for you serve the Lord Christ.*

I pray that your time reading this book has been a good experience. Perhaps you have learned something new or gained a better understanding about some particular point. At the least, what you have read may have been thought-provoking, which can lead you to more study.

I invite you to go to our Love Life Ministry website at lovelifeministry.com. There you will find devotions and teachings that you may want to read.

Should you have questions about what you have read in this book or what you read on our website, go to the SEEK page and send me or my wife Sandra your question. We will be happy to reply.

Closing Words

ARTWORK CREDIT LINE

Thomas Griffithe

Cover page art depicting abstract human body. Chapter preamble and header art depicting light burst. The color blue honors the priestly garments described in Exodus 28:31-38. Additional art graphics for spine and back cover for book titled "Vital Signs of Life in our Spirit."

IMAGE CREDIT LINE

R. Gino Santa Maria, Shutterfree, LLC, Dreamstime.com

Page vi image ID93558334 Jesus writing in the sand.

Homer L. Crothers, Ph.D. holds a doctorate in mathematical statistics from The Union Institute, Cincinnati, OH, and was employed as an international manufacturer consultant, managed the Statistics Department of Martin Marietta in Oak Ridge, TN., provided management improvement consulting to Wackenhut Security, Transnuclear Inc., and the Department of Energy. In his retirement, he attended and graduated from Charis Bible College-Atlanta, Georgia. Homer met his wife, Sandra, who was also a student at Charis Bible College. Upon graduation, as a married couple, they formed Love Life Ministry Inc. through which they minister to individuals who are struggling with life's issues. Together, Homer & Sandra have three children, eight grandchildren, and five great-grandchildren.

Be sure to visit Love Life Ministry Inc. website at lovelifeministry.com.

SALVATION PRAYER

If you have not received Jesus as your Savior, please pray the prayer below and become a child of God.

Lord Jesus, I have lived too long without You as my Savior.
I believe You are the Son of God.
I believe You died for my sin.
I believe You arose from the grave and are alive today.
I believe Your finished work was for me.

Therefore, I receive You as my Redeemer, Savior and Lord.

Thank You for giving me eternal life and filling my life with Your love.

Amen!

If you have prayed the Salvation Prayer, please let us know at info@lovelifeministry.com.

We welcome you into God's family.

READER'S REFLECTIONS

READER'S REFLECTIONS

READER'S REFLECTIONS

....

....

....

....

....

....

....

....

....

....

....

....

....

....

READER'S REFLECTIONS

....

....

....

....

....

....

....

....

....

....

....

....

....

....

Endnotes

END NOTES

CHAPTER 1

[1] Human Anatomy, 2nd Edition, Michael McKinley and Valerie Dean O'Loughlin, McGraw-Hill Higher Education, 2008, pp 127, 689, 745

[2] Ibid, pp 668, 675

[3] Ibid, pp 67

[4] Ibid, pp 95-108, 655, 760

[5] Ibid, pp 757-771

[6] Ibid, pp 759-763, 771, 746-748

[7] Ibid, pp 682

[8] Ibid, pp 120, 127, 637

[9] Regulation of Body Temperature by Autonomic and Behavioral Thermoeffectors, Zachary J. Schlader and Nicole T. Vargas, October 11, 2018, Center for Research and Education in Special Environments, Department of Exercise and Nutrition Sciences, University at Buffalo, Buffalo, NY 0091-6331/4702/116–126 Exercise and Sport Sciences Reviews DOI: 10.1249/JES.0000000000000180 Copyright © 2019 by the American College of Sports Medicine

CHAPTER 2

[10] Brown-Driver-Briggs Hebrew and English Lexicon, 14th. Printing, F. Brown, S. Driver, and C. Briggs, Hendrickson Publisher Marketing, LLC July 2012, Strong's number 3498

[11] Understanding Brain, Mind and Soul: Contributions from Neurology and Neurosurgery, Sunil K. Pandya, Copyright © Mens Sana Monographs, Jan-Dec 2011

[12] Location of the mind remains a mystery, LIFE, 22 August 2012, Douglas Heaven, New Scientist, https://www.newscientist.com/article/dn22205-location-of-the-mind-remains-a-mystery/#ixzz776fLwGb0

[13] Mind, Intelligence and Spirit, *Pascual F. Martínez-Freire, Universidad de Málaga,* tvgive@uma.es

[14] Center for Brains Minds + Machines, Course Number 9.S912, Instructors: Shimon Ullman, Tomaso Poggio, Massachusetts Institute of Technology (MIT), Fall 2012, hhttp://web.mit.edu/course/other/i2course/www.index.html

[15] Cell-cell interactions: How cells communicate with each other, Khan Academy, September 21, 2021

[16] The CONVERSATION, Academic Rigor, Journalistic Flair, October 23, 2019, https://theconversation.com/curious-kids-how-does-our-brain-send-signals-to-our-body-124950

[17] EMBO Reports "Mind-body research moves toward the mainstream," Vicki Brower, Copyright 2006, European Molecular Biology Organization

[18] Just How Much Power Does the Mind Have to Heal the Body? Melissa Dahl, FEB. 8, 2016

[19] * Name changed to protect privacy

CHAPTER 3

[20] Brown-Driver-Briggs Hebrew and English Lexicon, 14th. Printing, F. Brown, S. Driver, and C. Briggs, Hendrickson Publisher Marketing, LLC July 2012, Strong's number 3820

[21] THAYER'S GREEK-ENGLISH LEXICON OF THE NEW TESTAMENT, Joseph H. Thayer, Hendrickson Publishers Market, LLC, Peabody, Massachusetts 01961-3473, Strong's number 1343, 2014

[22] Present Truth magazine, Vol 37, Article 3, "The Righteousness of God," James E. Hanson

[23] Essential Cell Biology third edition; Bruce Alberts, Dennis Bray, Karen Hopkin, Alexander Johnson, Julian Lewis, Martin Raff, Keith Roberts, Peter Walter; Published by Garland Science, Taylor & Francis Group, LLC, New York, NY 10016, 2010, pp 388-407

[24] Ibid, pp 388-407

[25] Strong's Exhaustive Concordance of the Bible, Hebrew, and Chaldee Dictionary, James Strong, S.T.D., LL.D., 1976, Hebrew number 529

[26] Ibid, Greek Dictionary of the New Testament, Greek number 4102, 4100

[27] * Name changed to protect privacy

CHAPTER 4

[28] Human Anatomy, 2nd Edition, Michael McKinley and Valerie Dean O'Loughlin, McGraw-Hill Higher Education, 2008, pp 65

[29] Ibid pp 59

CHAPTER 5

[30] * Name changed to protect privacy

[31] Webmd.com, Parenting, Baby, Reference, The Benefits of Breastfeeding for Both Mother and Baby, September 2021

[32] Brown-Driver-Briggs Hebrew and English Lexicon, 14th. Printing, F. Brown, S. Driver, and C. Briggs, Hendrickson Publisher Marketing, LLC July 2012, Strong's number 1897

[33] Ibid, Strong's number 8451

CHAPTER 6

[34] Merriam-Webster 2021

[35] Ibid

[36] Ibid

[37] Ibid

[38] Ibid

[39] Ibid

[40] Joseph Prince Ministries Daily Grace Inspiration October 22 Bringing Every Thought Into Captivity

[41] * Name changed to protect privacy

[42] Ibid

[43] * Name change to protect privacy

[44] Cleveland Clinic, my.clevelandclinic.org/health/disease/15095-addisons-disease

[45] * Name changed to protect privacy

[46] * Name changed to protect privacy

[47] The Tongue-A Creative Force, Charles Capps, Capps Publishing, 1976, pages 70-73.

[48] Ibid

[49] God's Creative Power ® for Healing, Copyright © 1991 by Charles Capp, Published by Capps Publishing, page 4.

[50] * Name changed to protect privacy

[51] www.britannica.com/biography/Martin-Luther, June 6, 2019

[52] Herbert Bouman, "The Doctrine of Justification in the Lutheran Confessions," Concordia Theological Monthly 26 (November 1955) No. 11:801."Archived copy" (https://web.archive.o See also Further reading Notes rg/web/20080512021427/http://www.ctsfw.edu/library/files/pb/577). Archived from the original (http://www.ctsfw.edu/library/files/pb/577) on 2008-05-12. Retrieved 2009-03-15.

[53] Infusion and Imputation" An Introduction, Amy Mantravadi, Reformation 21, reformation21.org August 24, 2020

[54] https://en.wikipedia.org/w/index.php?title=Theology_of_Martin_Luther&oldid=1043412370" 10 September 2021

[55] Ibid

[56] The Walking Dead TV Series, created by Frank Darabont, www.amcplus.com

www.ingramcontent.com/pod-product-compliance
Lightning Source LLC
Chambersburg PA
CBHW060014050426
42448CB00012B/2746